NARROW

Preserving Fundamental Beliefs from Progressivism

BRANDON FOSTER

HIGH BRIDGE BOOKS
HOUSTON

Narrow
by Brandon Foster

Printed in the United States of America
ISBN (Paperback): 978-1-954943-48-3
ISBN (Hardcover): 978-1-954943-50-6

High Bridge Books titles may be purchased in bulk for educational, business, fundraising, or sales promotional use. For information, please contact High Bridge Books via www.HighBridgeBooks.com/contact.

Published in Houston, Texas by High Bridge Books

This book is dedicated to my amazing wife, Christina.
You are the reason why I embarked on this journey.

Contents

To Pam

Brandon Foster

1

The Beginning

> *Enter by the narrow gate. For the gate is wide and the way is easy that leads to destruction, and those who enter by it are many. For the gate is narrow and the way is hard that leads to life, and those who find it are few.*
>
> —Matthew 7:13–14 ESV

As with all beginnings, there must be an explanation as to why. Why was it written, and really why was it conceived? As for why this project was undertaken, I have one simple belief in life. That belief is that a person can only complain about something long enough before they either have to remain silent on the topic or do something about it.

That was the dilemma that I was in back at the end of 2020. I had been complaining about progressive Christianity for a while by that point, and I realized that I had reached my crossroad. As a believer in the Bible being the word of God, I had become annoyed at this popular group who claimed to follow God while simultaneously casting aside almost every aspect of His character and teaching. Many progressives believe things like the Bible is not God's infallible word, or they do not believe the idea that truth can be known.

Now I know that this is not the case for every progressive Christian. There are many out there who wrestle with Christianity because the church they grew up in or the pastor whom they dedicated their life to abandoned them. This is a sad reality both for the conservative Christian as well as the liberal. Too many pastors grow arrogant in their "leadership" of the church. Too many have caused pain leading more away from God than to Him. Now it is my belief that those who belong to God will always belong to Him, and those who have wandered will come back under His loving arms. But it is horrible to see and hear about these churches and the consequences. I do not want to invalidate the emotions and experiences of those who have lived through painful times. The leaders in the church who have caused pain or who have led many astray do need to be held accountable.

But, that is not the topic of this book. I also want to be clear that just because a person has experienced a traumatic event does not mean that the theology that they have drifted toward is correct. Many people who experience church trauma are hurt not by God or His theology but by man and his. In every story of church trauma I have heard, the person was hurt by extrabiblical theology and abusive people.

I hope that this book can be used as a shepherd's crook leading the straying sheep back to God. I am not arrogant enough to think that I know any better based on my own intellect. Everything I am and everything that I know is because of the grace of God. I thank Him every day for keeping me on His path, no matter how painful His corrections can be.[1]

This meant that as a believer who could be used as an instrument of healing and guiding, I had one of two choices. Either I had to accept that this was how the world was, or I had to do something to help guide people back to God's narrow path. I either had to remain silent and allow the wandering of my fel-

---

[1] More accurately, how painful my mistakes can be

low brothers and sisters, or I had to speak up and act like the lamp that I am called to be.[2] That is when I decided to write a book.

Now I am sure that you are wondering what kind of book you have picked up. You are also probably wondering why the book is titled *Narrow*. Those are both good questions. I will start with the title first. *Narrow* is referencing the concept from Matthew 7:13–14. God's path is narrow, not in how it treats the world, but in reference to how we live our lives. I know that is a little confusing so let me explain it like this. In life, we have many choices. We can categorize those choices in two ways. Either they are God's or the world's. If we desire to follow His ways, which lead to life, we have to follow His desires and decrees. When we follow Him, we walk down the narrow path. When we follow the world's advice, we travel down a wide path that will lead us to destruction. Unfortunately, life does not provide signs that inform us which path we are traveling. That is why I have written this book. God has shown us what He desires for us to stay on His road. Therefore, we only need to read His word, pray, and stay in Christian community, and we will be fine. Hopefully, this book will help as a navigational tool to differentiate between God's path and the world's path.

As for the second question, this book is a theological discussion on why progressive Christianity is incorrect both in action and in belief. They walk down the wide easy path, not God's narrow path. I have used the term above before, and I realize that it might need a small explanation. For those who are unsure of what a *progressive Christian* is, let me sum up the current popular trend. The quickest explanation is that a pro-

---

[2] "You are the light of the world. A city set on a hill cannot be hidden. Nor do people light a lamp and put it under a basket, but on a stand, and it gives light to all in the house. In the same way, let your light shine before others, so that they may see your good works and give glory to your Father who is in heaven." —Matthew 5:14–16 (ESV)

gressive Christian follows the current liberal, post-modern sway in thinking. I know there are some big concepts in that explanation, and I promise I will explain them more later, but for now, just know that progressives follow the current trend of the liberal side of culture. While being liberal is not inherently a bad thing, our culture has now swung the pendulum too far.

A more religious way of explaining progressive Christianity is that they stick closer to their political party[3] or cultural ideals[4] than to the Bible and Christ. To put it more bluntly, they follow Christ only as the last option or belief on a subject. This last part is for the most extreme cases. As said above, there are many fellow disciples who are genuinely confused. They have been given a lot of contradicting information in their life, and they are honestly trying to process it all. For those who are in this camp, I commend you as well as hope that this book helps. You are why I am writing this book. I know how confusing this world is, and I know that there are many beliefs being taught that all sound like they can be true. Sometimes we feel like the rope in tug-o-war. We are being pulled one way and then the other, and neither side seems to be winning, but we are just getting tired and feeling the pain.

The modern progressive believes many interesting things, but the worst one of them all is that they claim their beliefs are unique or original. I know that may sound a little harsh but hear me out. In my studies, I have learned that progressives are following almost step by step the beliefs held by an ancient cult called the Gnostics.

The Gnostics were a cultish group that reached their height during the early church.[5] So, why do I think that a group that

---

[3] This would be the Democratic Party at the moment.

[4] Acceptance of self-love, homosexual marriage, cancel culture, deconstruction, and scriptural dismantling to name a few.

[5] First to fourth centuries A.D.

died out centuries ago has been revived in the modern progressive? Well, here are the top similarities. Gnostics believed that they had secret revelations from God, and even if these revelations contradicted God, Scripture, or the apostles, it did not matter. Their revelations had precedent over these other sources.[6] They believed that they had an intimate relationship with God, and because of this, it was fine if their teachings contradicted who Christ appointed.[7] They claimed that there were more writings than the ones deemed canonical.[8,9] Because of this, they added new teachings that contradicted the apostles. They contradicted not only the apostles' teachings but the teachings of Christ as well. Basically, the Gnostics also chose the wide, easy path instead of the narrow path. They sought inclusion and acceptance over God's truth and love.

Some specific teachings of classic Gnostics were that Christ either did not come in the flesh,[10] but only in the spirit pretending to be corporeal, or he inhabited the body of a human and possessed him during his mission.[11] They also believed that since the physical world was evil, they did not have to sacrifice earthly pleasures because it was only the mind and spirit that mattered.[12] Another teaching was that sexual intimacy did not

---

[6] Rudolph, Kurt, and R Mcl Wilson. *Gnosis: The Nature and History of Gnosticism*. San Francisco, Harper & Row, 1987, p. 55.

[7] The apostles

[8] Rudolph, Kurt, and R Mcl Wilson. *Gnosis: The Nature and History of Gnosticism*. San Francisco, Harper & Row, 1987, pp. 44–48.

[9] The books we have in Scripture are deemed inspired by God and have gone through intensive scrutiny. Gnostics claimed that there were many more books, but these books could never pass the tests of holy inspiration.

[10] At that time, the physical world was considered evil.

[11] "Jesus Christ in Gnosticism—Gnosticism Explained." *Gnosticism Explained*, 22 May 2021, gnosticismexplained.org/jesus-christ-in-gnosticism/. Accessed 31 Mar. 2022.

[12] "The Gnostics and Jesus." *Monergism.com*, 2022,

need to be between only a man and a woman but that bisexuality was a holy thing.[13,14] They also twisted many biblical stories such as creation, the fall, and the need for a savior in general.[15]

The primary concept of Gnosticism, and why it was vehemently opposed by the church, was that God was either pure evil[16] or self-centered and should not be trusted. Obviously, this did not sit well with those who believed that Christ did come in the flesh and that God was a gracious, loving, benevolent God. These teachings can be found in the Gnostic gospels and other texts from the Nag Hammadi texts.

While not every teaching is the same, there are too many similarities to be ignored. It seems that each day, more and more Gnostic beliefs appear in sermons and on the internet. The main similarities lie in the idea of special revelation, Jesus not being the only way to heaven, that the Bible is not holy or inspired by God, and that the apostles taught incorrect theologies. These teachings forced other theologians to meet and debate over these heresies, and just like back then, it is happening again. Modern pastors are being forced to either combat these new ideas or join them.

Some progressives believe that they are fighting a battle that has never been fought before, meaning that they do not think the church has dealt with things like sexuality, defining truth, or why the Bible is the way that it is. This is not correct. One point of this book is to show that most, if not all, of the

---

www.monergism.com/thethreshold/articles/onsite/gnostics.html. Accessed 30 Mar. 2022.

13 ---. "Gnosticism a Basis for Same-Sex Marriage." *Eternity News*, Eternity News, 10 Aug. 2021, www.eternitynews.com.au/opinion/gnosticism-a-basis-for-same-sex-marriage/. Accessed 31 Mar. 2022.

14 Many of the deities in Gnostic mythology were bisexual.

15 Rudolph, Kurt, and R Mcl Wilson. *Gnosis: The Nature and History of Gnosticism*. San Francisco, Harper & Row, 1987, pp. 97, 99–100.

16 Since he created the physical world and the evils within.

progressive teachings are just recycled thoughts of ancient people claiming to be Christians. This does not inherently make them wrong, but it does deflate their balloon just a little.

Progressive Turned Neo-Gnostic

The modern progressive believes and teaches many of the same ideas as the Gnostics did. But I have said this already. Because of their many similarities, progressives will not be named progressives anymore. They will be called Neo-Gnostics because they are not progressing the church or theology. They are, in fact, moving it on a path of regression. I call them Neo-Gnostics because *neo* means new, and they are just Gnostics wrapped in a more modern package.

It is my hope to explain throughout this book the parallels between classic Gnosticism and Neo-Gnosticism. I am also going to try and show why their teachings are a regression not only theologically but also socially. What we believe becomes how we act. When we have wrong theology, as well as wrong beliefs about love, truth, charity,[17] and history, we are more apt to treat others incorrectly. These wrong things may not always be as extreme as stealing, adultery, or murder, but they will change how we treat others. That can be bad enough on its own.

My greatest hope is that my writings never come off as arrogant or too aggressive. It is my greatest hope and prayer that this book comes off humbly and filled with God's desires, not mine. Also, I understand how important tact can be when discussing controversial matters. Saying something humbly or aggressively can change the outcome of the conversation. There will be, of course, tough sections that might put some out of

[17] Charity is being used here in the classic form, as giving up not only money but also time.

their comfort zone. But I hope my tone does not take you off of God's path.

I believe that what we think becomes our outward actions. Because of this, if my arrogance is more evident than my love, that is a problem. As a disciple of Christ, it is my duty to share the gospel, fight the good fight, and run the good race. None of these things can be done if I am not walking the correct path. A large part of staying on God's path is how I am on the inside. God cares more about how we think and who we are on the inside. Again, this is because our actions are only the fruit of our thoughts. This is what Jesus was getting at in Matthew 5:21–22 and 27–28. The thought of hate or lust was just as bad as the action toward God.

As Matthew wrote in the verse above, if the gate is narrow, the path will be as well. John Bunyan, the Puritan preacher, describes it well in his book *The Pilgrim's Progress* by showing over and over again the main characters failing to stay on the road. All too often, they wandered off the road because they were following what they thought were good intentions. But our good intentions may not always be God's. It is very hard to stay on the straight, narrow path prescribed by God. That is why he guides us. If I am to do my duty to Him, I have to be in continual meditation on His word.

It is my hope that this book will help guide some back to God. No book should be treated on the same level as God's holy Word, especially not this one. But it is still my hope that this book can be used by God. This book's purpose is to argue for the beliefs held by disciples of Christ. I do not want this book to become a stand-alone book nor a book read without reading Scripture first. I humbly hope this book helps you on your journey to and with Christ. Let us now begin walking the narrow path following God together.

2

Ideology

Everyone then who hears these words of mine and does them will be like a wise man who built his house on the rock. And the rain fell, and the floods came, and the winds blew and beat on that house, but it did not fall, because it had been founded on the rock.

—Matthew 7:24–25 ESV

Here we stand at our trail's beginning. This, like most paths that deal with life-altering concepts, is not a path to be taken lightly, nor can it be traveled down by our own strength. This can only be done through God's strength and by His direction. Therefore, on His strength alone, let the journey begin.

Standing at this first crossroad, we can see dozens of trails leading off in many different directions. Each road leads to a different destination, which is why it is important which path one takes. This is because only one can lead to the correct destination. Every other path will lead to nothing or damnation. Who knows how many crossroads each road contains? But only one road can lead to God.

Some have pretty trees lining the path, others have immense stonework erected, and still others are old and worn, showing signs of the number of travelers they have seen. Each trail is different. Some trails look pretty at the beginning, but they have nothing more to them. Others have what seem to be strong pillars that can protect their travelers. But they actually offer no protection. And still others are so worn that their meaning has been lost to time.

This first intersection concerns beliefs. Obviously, if we do not understand what we believe, we cannot understand how we will react to the world around us. Also, our worldview is the thing that we build everything else on. Our outward actions are just the visible commands of our inward thoughts and beliefs.[1] Therefore, to understand why we do things, we should first investigate what we believe.

Too many individuals believe that they have an open mind when, in all reality, they follow a set of beliefs just like anyone else. Everyone has some form of a belief system, whether they admit to it or not. Because of this, we need to discuss in general details[2] belief systems, also called worldviews or ideologies,[3] and how they affect life.

Beliefs, like most things in this life, can be both simple and complex. To be honest, this duality makes them difficult to discuss. A belief can be like a simple pond discovered in a forest. It seems shallow from above; calm and inviting ripples slowly cross the surface. But when an individual takes a dive, they dis-

---

[1] Please do not get annoyed with that phrase yet; it will be said many more times throughout this book.

[2] Sadly, one chapter cannot truly satisfy this topic completely. It has required years of study in history and politics for others to tackle this issue. But let it suffice to say that this chapter is not trying to explain ideology completely but rather how it interplays with Christianity and Neo-Gnosticism.

[3] Ideologies are a type of belief system that encompasses an entire person's life or a large part of it.

cover that it is deep with many hidden beliefs lying within. Those that remain on the surface will never know the beauty, or the horror, that lurks beneath. Some beliefs are calm and peaceful up top, while their depths are deadly. An example of this would be Neo-Gnosticism. At first, their ideas about love, truth, and charity sound welcoming and good. But as their beliefs are explored, they become dark, bitter, and angry. Others are calm on both the surface as well as at its depths. This would be Christianity. It teaches us to love one another at the surface, and the deeper we dive, the more we find love.

As we live through life, we cannot remain on the pond's surface. There are too many problems in this world for us to remain naive. Naivety in childhood is fine, but naivety in adulthood produces individuals who allow evils to grow. We can be naive when we are children, but we all must take responsibility for our lives and our beliefs when we reach the age of maturity.

To be fair, reaching maturity is a difficult thing to define. Some cultures claim adulthood is reached at thirteen, while others may say sixteen. In American society, adulthood is reached at the age of eighteen. The term maturity is meant more on the physical side. We are deemed mature by society when we reach adulthood. Mental maturity is an entirely different thing. There are people who are in their teens who are more mature than some in their eighties.

Another reason to discuss ideologies is that they do and do not pertain to religion. Confusing, right? Ideologies, at their base nature, do not pertain to religions, yet they tend to replace religion. Again, this is confusing, but it should make sense by the end. The modern ideology of the Neo-Gnostic world has tried to replace the traditional religious base of their parents. This is why ideologies have been so powerful. People used to flock to churches, temples, or mosques to feel purpose in life. Now they have replaced those institutions with a new institution. This is the institution of self. This is why we have self-love, my-truth, subjectivity, and selfishness rampant in our culture.

This is not a step toward progress but a regression toward individualistic tribalism.[4] We are seeing the effects of this all over the Western world and in America specifically. Instead of viewing ourselves as American, we now have broken up as Democrat or Republican, white or colored, male or female, straight or LGBTQIA+, and the list is continually growing as every year passes.

Primarily, the difference between an ideology and a traditional religion is that ideologies pertain more to the political sphere and to the here and now. Their end-all-be-all is to perfect this world through political regulation or manipulation. An ideology desires to reform this life without much thought for the afterlife. While religions do try to reform this world, their main objective is the afterlife. Either way, religion does not use politics to achieve its goals.[5] This is a key point when it comes to the Neo-Gnostic movement. Disciples of Christ use spiritual reform to change the heart. A changed heart will lead to social and political reform. Neo-Gnostics use political policies to change the heart. The problem is that people do not change based on a law. Laws do not stop actions; they only create consequences for those actions. To change a person's actions, we need to change their heart.

---

[4] Tribalism is the idea of belonging to a specific group and defending that group fiercely because it is yours. Usually, tribalistic mentalities turn aggressive or violent toward anything or anyone different. Tribalism hates the "other" passionately and wishes all things to be within the tribe's sphere.

[5] While religion does not use politics, politics has used religion. Many politicians, kings, and local magistrates have used religion to achieve their ends. This has happened on every continent under every religion. For those under the intoxication of power, religion has proven to be a reliable source to rise quickly.

Building a Solid Foundation

To truly understand how ideologies work, let us use the concept of a construction site. Before construction can begin on any site, a few things have to happen. First, the rubble or overgrowth must be cleared, then it must be leveled, and lastly, the foundation has to be built. No architects will skip any of these steps if they are worth their salt. This is because each step is important and leads to the next one. If a step is skipped, then the next step becomes drastically more difficult or even impossible. Say that the landscape was not cleared. How difficult would it be to level the land if the ground could not even be seen? Some ground is so overgrown that vines, bushes, and marshy terrain cover every inch. It would be impossible to complete steps two or three without the land being cleared. Therefore, each step is done in sequence. But once this long process is finished and the architect is satisfied with the site, the next phase can begin. Now the ground can be leveled and compacted.

This may sound simple in practice but can be very difficult in execution. Land either must be raised by depositing dirt, gravel, and sand, or it must be lowered by removing earth. Either way, it takes time, energy, and patience to level a field. Obviously, the bigger the field, the more time it is going to take. As dirt is either removed or added, the ground must be continually compacted. This is especially important when the ingredients above are added. They tend to be loose, and as they are spread across the field, they must be compacted through continual pressure. There are specific machines designed to apply pressure to turn loose dirt into compacted earth.

The last thing to do is lay the actual foundation. Out of all three, this is the most important. While each step does build upon the step before it, this step is the climax of the equation.

For the rest of the building to be strong, the foundation must be built strong. A weak foundation results in a weak building. Normal foundations are usually around a few feet deep, but buildings that tower above the ground[6] have foundations that can go hundreds of feet down. The higher the building goes up, the deeper the foundation.

To build towering structures like those found in New York, Shanghai, or London, their foundation must be exceedingly deep and strong.[7] None of these steel goliaths can stand if their foundations are weak. The building itself might be made well, but a weak foundation will ruin everything above.

Building the Intellectual Foundation

The intellectual building we will be discussing was first formed at the birth of the individual. As we grow up and start to develop beliefs, our building starts to form. The initial forming starts with parents. They teach us how to walk, talk, and act. Hopefully, this is done carefully and through intentional moments. This formation heavily depends on the family and community of the individual. Those who grow up in loving, supportive families and communities tend to have stronger foundations than those who lack these things.[8]

With that said, there are still many individuals who grow up with their parents trying to create a strong foundation for them who still end up with a weak foundation. This is because the one who grew up in a good home chose incorrect beliefs, or the one who grew up poorly chose wise ones. While we are influenced by those around us, it is ultimately our decision on

---

[6] Like a skyscraper

[7] They are also built with different material to strengthen the building. They use steel poles driven into the ground with concrete around them to form an unmovable base. This allows the buildings to be anchored and never move, minus the slight swaying that is normal for skyscrapers.

[8] This is not always the case, though.

what we believe. A person in a poor environment can still make good decisions, and a person in a good environment can make bad ones. That is not to say that we should not try and create the best environment for our children. Those who grow up in good environments have a drastically higher chance of making good decisions.

If poor ideologies are chosen, both groups will usually face ideological stagnation. This stagnation leads them to have simple beliefs and stunted maturity. This is when the building starts to go into disrepair and is in need of a total renovation. When a building has received enough damage, it has to be fixed at the foundational level before the building above can be fixed. If a person's worldview is shattered entirely, they will need a new ideologic foundation before they can start tackling the smaller things in life. This is why we need Christ and the transforming grace that He provides.

Deconstructing Beliefs

Developing a strong ideology is complementary to constructing or repairing a building. Some individuals are so broken that as they try to reconstruct their life, they have difficulty finding beliefs they can trust. Everything that they knew, or that they thought they knew, has broken down. Because of this, they are in need of constructing a new foundation more than they are in need of repairing an old one.

A child entering the age of maturity will be more like a home repair. Some repairs are as drastic as the one mentioned above, but most are just small repairs that help improve the home. As children grow, they develop beliefs and opinions based on their parents, friends, and other adults around them. They also learn from TV shows, video games, websites, and apps. There are a plethora of ways children are influenced in today's world. Because of all these sources, our building of beliefs becomes overcrowded, and it desperately needs to be fixed up and expanded.

Once they reach the age of maturity, individuals should start to ponder life for themselves. All the beliefs acquired during childhood are like a building in an overgrown field. Nothing makes sense, and everything is wild and a little broken. This is partly because children believe the most outrageous things. Outside of the normal beliefs of Santa Clause, the Easter Bunny, and the Tooth Fairy, children believe in odd, obscure things. It is hard to give examples of their beliefs because of their variety, but ask any child what they believe about a topic, and eventually, they will say something mind-boggling.

Most of our childhood beliefs are based more on our parents' beliefs (faith and worldly) than on our own.[9] As we grow, naturally our parents teach and guide us. This is normal and good. Parents are supposed to be the first and primary guides in our lives. But parents, like everyone else, are fallible. Therefore, it is important to reevaluate one's beliefs to double-check their teachings. Having an overgrown field of beliefs is fine when we are young, but we must take control of our beliefs once we reach the age of maturity.

There is a modern term that sums up the reevaluation period well. This term is *deconstruction*. Deconstruction does have a lot of negative connotations in the modern Western world due to how it is used by most people. This is because many Neo-Gnostics, as well as progressives in general, use this term as a way to excuse their prideful belief that they know better than those before them.[10] Instead of truly studying the debated topic

---

[9] Though, as we said, there can be many other contributors.

[10] As stated in the introduction, there are many deconstructionists who do not fall into this classification. They are deconstructing because their world has shattered for one reason or another. Those who fall into this category are not being discussed in this paragraph. Those who dislike God's ways because they deem their ways better than His are the focal point of this section. They deliberately turn their head so that they can avoid God.

from different angles, they tend to gravitate toward the opposing side and believe their argument at face value. It is not good to blindly follow a belief or to abandon it without considering the belief completely.

As the word implies, deconstruction is the concept of taking an idea and breaking it down to its foundation. Deconstruction done correctly is a common practice that has been utilized for centuries. The Reformation, the Scientific Revolution, and the Enlightenment were all deconstructionist movements. They desired to find the truth no matter the cost.

Martin Luther deconstructed the beliefs of the Catholic church. Isaac Newton deconstructed the perceived laws of science. Thomas Payne deconstructed the political and philosophical beliefs of Europe. The modern issue is that many deconstructionists do not actually do the research required. The three men mentioned above dedicated their lives to research, not just to an opinion. Modern deconstructionists tend to reevaluate their lives through feelings, experiences, and some reading. This has caused a lot of issues because individuals are flocking to specific beliefs not because they have been proven to be true but because they are contrary to a belief that they do not like. Or, to put it another way, Neo-Gnostics dislike a way of thinking so bad that they are willing to adopt any other belief without contemplating the depths of that belief.[11]

---

[11] Primarily, Neo-Gnostics dislike traditional Christian beliefs and practices, so they have adopted many modern progressive beliefs. While some of these beliefs started as good concepts decades ago, they have turned into the very thing that they hated in the first place. Most of the beliefs that Neo-Gnostics are flocking to have a long history, meaning that there is a lot of sources to research. But most have chosen to forsake this research because they feel like the belief is good. Beliefs such as the goodness of man, the acceptance of sin, and the belief that all religions lead to God have all been practiced before. Neo-Gnostics believe that their way of thinking is new and revolutionary because they do not understand history.

A good example of deconstruction is baptism. As we have said before, deconstruction is researching a belief all the way down to its base or core. This is done to see if it is good, true, or being done correctly. Part of this is to also study why it is practiced. There are many different views on any subject, and it is good to see what the other side believes. Catholics practice one form of baptism, Protestants another, Baptists yet another, and the list goes on for every denomination out there. Each one has a slightly different understanding of baptism or how to do it. It is good to read Scripture to see which practice is correct or if there is even an issue with so many different forms of Baptismal practices.

There are other beliefs[12] that hold no scriptural validity. Scripture speaks clearly that Jesus is God.[13, 14] It does not require much research to understand Jesus's claims of divinity. This is another prime deconstruction topic. This, unlike baptism, is a central belief in Christianity. If an individual is claiming to be a believer in Christ, yet they do not understand what Scripture says about Him, how can they truly know what they believe?

Deconstructing the Flood

The key to deconstruction is study. To truly deconstruct something, that supposed truth needs to be fully researched, pondered, and as fully understood as possible. An individual cannot claim to be deconstructing their faith by studying only atheistic sources. A person who is truly trying to find truth

---

[12] Like Jesus being a god, not part of the Trinity

[13] "…that they may all be one, just as you, Father, are in me, and I in you, that they also may be in us, so that the world may believe that you have sent me." —John 17:21 (ESV)

[14] Matthew 2:1-2, 28:8–9, 28:19; John 1:1, 1:14, 1:18, 5:18, 8:57–58, 10:30, 10:33, 13:18–19; Acts 7:59–60; Philippians 2:5–6; Colossians 2:9–10; 1 Corinthians 8:6; 1 John 5:20

needs to study that topic to see what learned Christians in that field have to say and then study the atheistic sources. Or vice-versa; it does not really matter.

Another scriptural story besides Jesus's life that has come under a lot of scrutiny in the last century or two is the Genesis flood. This is a great example because it has scientific and historical evidence to study. Jesus can only be researched through Scripture and some historical documentation.[15] The flood was a global catastrophe that can be seen through many disciplines. We have archeological, historical, anthropological, and religious documentation or stories that deal with a global flood.

This is a common biblical story that starts creating the wedge for Neo-Gnostics because modern science says it never happened. This seed of doubt grows into Neo-Gnostics questioning every Christian belief through a secular lens.

The deconstruction thought goes something like this: "I was taught about the flood as a child, and I never thought much of it. Recently, I took a science class at my school, and they taught that the story of the biblical flood is wrong. They said that it is impossible because the world has been undergoing something called uniformitarianism,[16] and no global catastrophes have occurred since the death of the dinosaurs. They also taught us that the fossil record does not support any of the claims in the Bible. I have been thinking a lot about this, and my pastor has not really helped. I am really confused about this,

---

[15] The historical documents only state that He lived and that He died the way the Bible says He did. No historical document can prove His statements of divinity or His ascension. We are left completely up to the mercy of Scripture here.

[16] The theory is that changes in the earth's crust during geological history have resulted from the action of continuous and uniform processes. It is often contrasted with catastrophism.

but I guess since science says it did not happen, I don't believe in the flood anymore."

This is a generic statement that sums up some of the points that individuals make as they travel down this path. It is very true that modern science does not support many of the claims stated in the Bible. But modern science also does not support many of its own claims. There are too many examples of contradictions in geology alone that truly explain why blindly trusting science is foolish.

There are fossils and other geological findings that show human footsteps in the same strata as dinosaurs or other animals that were supposed to have lived millions of years before humans. [17] Evolutionists believe that mankind emerged around one million years ago in the late tertiary period. Yet, some large human footprints have been found in rocks believed to be in the Carboniferous Period, which was about two hundred fifty million years ago. [18] This is not a small difference in time. There are also too many examples of this to make it a fluke. Scientists cannot explain why an overabundance of human footprints has been found in strata where no human evidence should be found.

Science is not perfect, and it needs to be acknowledged that it is a work in progress. We do not understand everything about the universe, and we never will. This means that it cannot be trusted at the same level as God. What a person needs to do during their period of deconstruction is find reliable sources that discuss their topic and research them. Find well-researched books on the flood and see how other disciples defend the biblical account. Research why secularists disagree with the flood, and after enough data has been collected, reevaluate. If the be-

---

[17] Whitcomb and Morris. "The Genesis Flood." *The Presybyterian and Reformed Publishing Company*. 1967. pp. 172–173.

[18] Whitcomb and Morris. "The Genesis Flood." *The Presybyterian and Reformed Publishing Company*. 1967. pp. 172–173.

lief is true, it will stand up. If it is not true, well, it will not. There is enough evidence proving the existence of a global catastrophe to say that the story of the biblical flood is true. There is also enough doubt on the scientific side to say that they do not always know what they are talking about.

Reconstructing Beliefs

As we search through our library of beliefs, there comes a time to test which ones can withstand scrutiny. This is like clearing out the foliage around a house. As beliefs that are no longer desired are cleared away, it leaves room for our foundation to be formed or fixed. To use the popular metaphor, "one's cup has to be emptied before it can be refilled." A cup that is already full of ideologies has no room to add more. One's cup level must be continually lowered and filled again to not become stagnant. Stagnant water becomes full of algae, bacteria, and filth, making those around it sick.

In construction, the clearing and the leveling happen in two distinct phases. In ideologic study, they happen more simultaneously. As a belief is being deconstructed (the clearing phase), it is then being reconstructed (the leveling phase). This reconstruction can either be strong or weak, depending on the amount of study. As our building is being cleared, the beliefs that remain have more room. This extra room allows for more beliefs that are similar to be displayed as well. This widens and deepens our beliefs and understandings of life.

Proof Produces Strength

Intellectual foundations are exactly the same as those on a construction site. They must be deep and strong so that the rest of life can rest on them. There are many different ideologies out in the world, and many of them cannot support the complexities of reality. This is because their foundations are weak and crumble at the first tremor of life. While there are many ideologies in general, there are only a few major ideologies. These major ideologies[19] are the foundations for all other beliefs. If a weak one is chosen, then a weak foundation is cast. If a strong ideology is chosen, then a strong foundation is built, and a tall building can be constructed.

There are many beliefs out in this world, and many of them have no proof of their validity. This lack of proof makes them weak. Weak beliefs (foundations) create weak minds (stunted buildings). A short building can only be built on a weak foundation, and even this type of building has a high chance of being blown away with any breeze. No one should want to live in a small, weak house.

History of Ideologies

Therefore, the discussion of ideology is a must for anyone trying to live as a mature person or disciple of Christ. The definition of ideology is any wide-ranging system of beliefs, ways of thought, and categories that provide the foundation of programs of political and social action: an ideology is a conceptual scheme with a practical application.[20] Whatever ideology one believes creates the foundation for everything else. As the Oxford definition states above, ideologies are what produce social and political application. In other words, everything one does (whether it is in politics or in their day-to-day life) stems from their ideology.

The concept of ideology stems from a man named Antoine Destutt de Tracy. He was an eighteenth to nineteenth-century

---

[19] Also called primary ideologies

[20] Oxford Reference. 2021. *ideology*. [online] Available at: <https://www.oxfordreference.com/view/10.1093/oi/authority.20110803095956722> [Accessed 18 August 2021].

French politician who is known for forming the term ideology,[21] which means "science of ideas." He lived during the French revolution and the reign of Napoleon I. His definition of ideology went as such: "(1) it contains an explanatory theory of a more or less comprehensive kind about human experience and the external world; (2) it sets out a program, in generalized and abstract terms, of social and political organization; (3) it conceives the realization of this program as entailing a struggle; (4) it seeks not merely to persuade but to recruit loyal adherents, demanding what is sometimes called commitment; (5) it addresses a wide public but may tend to confer some special role of leadership on intellectuals." Or in a loose definition "ideology may mean any kind of action-oriented theory or any attempt to approach politics in the light of a system of ideas."[22] While de Tracy may not have incorporated religion into his realm of ideology, it can be argued that religion is a form of ideology. It fits the loose definition and many of his points as well.

Religion is an action-oriented theory that has a system of ideas. The only point that religion does not fit well within de Tracy's definition would be point two. Religion does usually set out to create a political or social organization. This does tend to happen because mankind is socially and politically minded, but religion usually desires to set up a set of behaviors to usher an individual into the good place in the afterlife. Religion focuses more on ethics, morals, and the good vs. evil of an individual, while ideology focuses on the system and society as a whole. This seems like a small difference, but in practice, this difference becomes very clear.

Take traditional Christianity and Neo-Gnosticism. Christians do participate in social and political construction, but that is not the point of Christianity. The point of Christianity is

---

[21] Idéologie in French

[22] Cranston, Maurice. "Ideology | Society." Encyclopædia Britannica, 27 Nov. 2014, www.britannica.com/topic/ideology-society.

Christ and the work that He did for His creation and glory. On the other hand, Neo-Gnosticism is more about social and political reform than about Christ or living a life for God. Also, since these two beliefs have differing opinions on the condition of man's heart, the root of evil, and the way to solve the world's problems, their outward expressions are very different. Some Christians might try to influence others to do good through political means,[23] but there are many other ways that they try to better their communities. Political reform tends to be very low on their list.[24] Many Neo-Gnostics only desire political and social change, but they do not put much effort on their own part to accomplish these goals. They might do little things here and there, but when it comes to sacrificially serving, there is very little effort.

Religion and Politics

There is an argument that religion needs to stay out of politics. Simultaneously, the same people argue that politics needs to get into religion. The argument claims that one's religious views should not influence their votes. The problem is that if religion is a type of ideology, then it cannot be separated from any aspect of our lives. Religions have teachings for every part of a person's life. Therefore, it can be classified as a primary ideology.

---

[23] Not taxing churches so that they can contribute more to charities, allowing charitable donations to be tax write-offs, or punishing individuals who steal, murder, or cheat

[24] Though as people become less involved in the church, their reformation tendencies also decline. Those not gripped by the transformation of Christ tend to focus more on themselves than on serving and saving others. Because of this, many church attending individual have accepted the practice of just voting the sins away. Instead of cleaning up their own communities, they have become perfectly fine with letting the government do it for them.

The argument for separating religion from politics is ridiculous. If religion is a primary ideology, then it is impossible to keep its tendrils out of politics. Christianity speaks on almost every aspect of life specifically and the rest by inference. This means that it is impossible to separate any ideology from other aspects of life. Modern secularism is also a primary ideology. It is exactly like a religion, and the god being worshiped is the Self.

Over the last two centuries, secularism[25] has replaced or reshaped traditional religions. While secularism is the rejection of religion, it is itself a form of religion. This means that when secularists tell believers that they cannot vote through their faith, secularists need to be informed that they are voting through their faith. Both are the same.

Strong Foundation

If all major belief systems are a type of ideology, then they cannot be accepted or taken lightly. Weak ideologies produce weak, bitter people. Strong ideologies produce courageous, loving people. The foundation of a building allows for the strength of the building. If the ideological foundation is weak, then the beliefs built upon it will be weak. A weak foundation can only hold a small building. A small building can only hold a small number of rooms.[26] Therefore, a weak ideology cannot deal with many varied situations in life. This is why some ideologies, like Neo-Gnosticism, tend to use the same answer for multiple situations.

---

[25] Indifference to or rejection or exclusion of religion and religious considerations. "Merriam-Webster Dictionary." *Merriam-Webster.com*, 2022, www.merriam-webster.com/dictionary/secularism. Accessed 2 May 2022.

[26] Rooms are the spaces that hold varied situations in life. Thus a small building cannot hold the variety of situations life will present.

One example of this is the emphasis on identity. An identity is how one sees themselves. This concept may be contrary to reality or science, but that does not matter because identity relies more on the internal thoughts of the person. So, a man can identify as a woman, a white person can be black, a fifty-five-year-old can be six, or any other combination imagined. For many Neo-Gnostics, the issue in the world is not sin nor the evilness of man[27] but the fact that individuals have not been allowed to identify as they wished. Their thinking is that if social restrictions were lifted, people's natural goodness would overcome their biases, and the world would turn to peace.

All of mankind's issues are boiled down to one problem that can be fixed through one solution. Neo-Gnostics believe that the goodness of man is only suppressed by social and governmental constructs. This means that if man is freed from these oppressive institutions, their pure goodness will shine.[28]

Life is too complicated to try and fit all its issues into one room. Neo-Gnostics are correct when they claim that there are social, racial, gender, and class issues in the world. It is very clear that men and women can be very cruel to each other, that different ethnic groups can hate another for any number of reasons, that society can be cruel, and that classes treat those below or above them with contempt. These issues are not being debated. Almost every ideology perceives the same ills in life. The problem is that each one has a different way of dealing with them. Stronger ideologies differentiate one problem from another, and this allows them to create different solutions. Unlike

---

[27] Jeremiah 17:9, Psalms 58:3, Genesis 6:5, Jeremiah 13:23, Romans 3:10–11, Romans 7:18, Ephesians 4:8, and Romans 3:12

[28] This is ignoring the fact that institutions are created and sustained by people. Therefore, if an institution is evil, those who created it and keep it running would be evil. Evil people make evil systems. We cannot remove the blame for evilness by shifting it from the hearts of man and putting it into some vague systematic structure.

how Neo-Gnostics try to boil every issue down to an identity issue, Christians sort each problem by room and deal with that room specifically. Life is a complicated set of actions and reactions; thus, not every issue can be dealt with by using the same solution. No one solution fixes every issue. At least not from mankind's side of existence.[29]

The foundation for disciples is Christ and His word. Everything a disciple believes is built on the teachings of Christ and Scripture. This is summarized by the verse at the beginning of this chapter.

Matthew writes that those who follow His[30] words[31] will be able to withstand any storm. But those who ignore His words will be like living in a house built on sand. Those who have observed waves on sand will know that the ocean moves the sand around easily. This means that the foundation on a beach will be quickly weakened, and the house will crumble. When a modern house is built on a beach, it is built either on the rock below the sand (if the rock is close enough) or on cement blocks. Buildings constructed directly on the sand cannot withstand any mild or harsh environments.

Christ may be specifically speaking about His teachings, but His words can be applied to all ideologies. As stated above, a strong foundation allows the building to withstand any storm. Those who follow the teachings of Christ can withstand any hardship in life. We receive perseverance, hope, grace, love, and peace from Christ, and this allows us to deal with life's hardships.

---

[29] From God's perspective, there is only one solution: Himself. As origin, sustainer, and savior, He is the only thing that can fix our world.

[30] Christ's

[31] Which is Scripture

Belief and Believer

Everyone has a belief that acts as the foundation for the rest of their life, though sometimes they may not know it or admit to it. Everyone has something that they base most, if not all, their life on. For many, this might be a subconscious belief, and for others, it is a very conscious one. What matters when it comes to these conscious or subconscious beliefs is not the believer or the strength of their belief but the belief itself. A weak belief will never stand to the realities of life. Life can be very cruel sometimes, and if an individual places their faith in one of these weak ideologies, they will not be able to perceive those trials. There have been many beliefs throughout history that, once tested, completely failed and quickly faded away.

There are those who believe that if they believe hard enough, good things will happen. They think God will answer their prayer because they prayed it hard enough,[32] or they think that the universe will manifest it for them. Usually, these individuals become bitter and depressed when their desires are not rewarded. A person can believe wholeheartedly in something, but if it is false, it does not matter. Their belief, no matter how strong, amounts to nothing. A weak faith in a strong belief is better than a strong faith in a weak belief. This is why Christ says if only we had the strength of a mustard seed.[33]

This statement occurs right after the disciples had failed to heal a boy possessed by a demon.[34] This is something that they

---

[32] God does answer prayers, and we are commanded to pray. The difference here is that we are praying for more selfish desires, and those God rarely answers.

[33] He said to them, "Because of your little faith. For truly, I say to you, if you have faith like a grain of mustard seed, you will say to this mountain, 'Move from here to there,' and it will move, and nothing will be impossible for you." —Matthew 17:20 (ESV)

[34] Matthew 17:14–16

had seen Christ do,[35] yet they still lacked the faith to accomplish it themselves. This is why Christ states that if we only possess faith the size of a mustard seed, we could do great things. Their seeds are the tiniest, yet they can grow into giant plants. Mustard seeds are about one to two millimeters in size[36] but can grow into a bush six to twenty feet tall with a twenty-foot width. Some extraordinary plants can get to thirty feet tall.[37]

In essence, Christ is saying that a small amount of faith can lead to an incredible life in God. Christ knew that the average person could hardly produce any faith, but it did not matter because the belief itself was what mattered. Christ is what mattered because He would do the rest. We just need to put an iota of faith in Him.

To use another example, there was an ancient study called alchemy. This was a medieval study that believed that one material could be turned into another. Primarily they desired to turn iron into gold, cure disease, and prolong life.[38] This is where the concept of the philosopher's stone and searching for eternal life comes from. This practice sounds nice, right? Well, the problem is that after centuries, alchemy still has not come up with anything.

An individual could believe with all their might, but it would not matter. Natural philosophers[39] have shown after centuries of experimentation that this type of molecular manipulation is impossible. They truly believed that it was possible to

---

[35] Matthew 8:16 and 9:32–33 for more examples in Matthew

[36] "Are Mustard Seeds the Smallest or Was Jesus Wrong?" *Answers in Genesis*, answersingenesis.org/bible-questions/are-mustard-seeds-the-smallest-or-was-jesus-wrong/.

[37] "Will Small Lime Bushes Bear Fruit?" *Home Guides | SF Gate*, homeguides.sfgate.com/small-lime-bushes-bear-fruit-59472.html.

[38] "Definition of alchemy." *Merriam-Webster.com*, 2019, www.merriam-webster.com/dictionary/alchemy.

[39] The term used for scientists during the Middle Ages and Renaissance

turn one object into something else. They believed with complete conviction, but their belief did not matter. Reality cannot be changed even through the strength of belief.

A better term here might be faith. Faith[40] in the wrong thing produces nothing but frustration. There are some things in life that cannot be proven outright. Some natural phenomena cannot be seen, but their effects can be felt. One common example is the wind. The wind has never been seen, but we see what the wind does every day. We see it rustle leaves, brush across one's face, or obliterate a house. Each is an example of the effects of the wind, yet the wind is never actually seen. Dirt, leaves, or other debris can signal where the wind is blowing, but it itself is still never seen. Because of this, we have faith that the wind exists because we feel it and see its effects. Faith is not a bad thing, but just like belief, faith in the wrong thing can be devastating.

These two examples not only show that the belief is more important than the believer but also that what one believes can carry into other aspects of life. No belief is isolated. Every belief has lines that connect it to other beliefs. This is why ideologies are important to understand and study as deeply as possible.

Consumption

Being consumed means "completely fill the mind of."[41] Or in other words, being consumed means that a person has no action that does not somehow relate to another action. All aspects of life can be connected to one ideology. This can be a bad thing or a good thing. It can be bad if the ideology pushes the individual toward hate. An example of this type of ideology would be social Darwinism.

---

[40] The belief in something unseen

[41] "Consume | Definition of Consume by Oxford Dictionary on Lexico.com Also Meaning of Consume"

Social Darwinism is the belief that mankind is in an evolutionary struggle, and it is up to the strong to propel the species into a higher stratus of existence. This term was first coined by Joseph Fisher in 1877.[42] Ironically, this term has Darwin's name, yet he most likely would have disliked the theory. This theory follows ideologues such as Herbert Spencer,[43] Thomas Malthus,[44] and Francis Galton.[45] This was also a popular ideology that led to World War I, World War II, modern racism, and in more recent decades, critical race theory. This ideology has led to drastic social divide and should be put to rest. This is more of a secondary ideology that rests under evolutionary atheism. The individuals who follow this ideology are consumed by its teachings, and every aspect of their lives is attached to it. Their political, environmental, societal, and psychological beliefs all start to become entangled in this belief.

An example of another secondary ideology would be the "good Samaritan." This ideology taught by Christ is the idea of loving and helping others no matter their religious practices, their ethnicity, or their economic status. The Samaritan in this story helps a Jew who had been beaten while traveling between two cities.[46] He not only binds his wounds, but he also transports him to an inn and pays for everything. This man, who would have disliked the Jews,[47] overcame his hate and showed love and compassion for his enemy. Just like the first example,

---

[42] Kiprop, Victor. "What Is Social Darwinism?" *WorldAtlas*, WorldAtlas, 15 Nov. 2017, www.worldatlas.com/articles/what-is-social-darwinism.html. Accessed 2 May 2022.

[43] Nineteenth-century philosopher, sociologist, and author who coined the phrase *survival of the fittest*

[44] Eighteenth-century author who started the population control theory

[45] Author who some believed coined the term *eugenics*

[46] Who had cultural, religious, and ethnic differences

[47] And vice versa

this ideology, which is also a secondary ideology, also consumes the individual. His belief in love and mercy overcame his distaste because love consumed him.

One ideology has led to the death and destruction of millions, while the other has led to love and healing. One is full of hate, the other full of love. One was taught by secular liberalism, the other by Christianity.

Transformation

While an individual can be consumed by any ideology, they can only be transformed by one. This type of change is drastically different from the one mentioned above. Being consumed can happen to anyone in any ideology. Being transformed can only happen to those who are radically changed by the power of Christ.

There are stories after stories of individuals going from grotesque individuals mentally (racists, philanderers, and misogynists, to name a few) to loving, happy people who care and help people. There have been murderers who have had a complete personality change after experiencing Christ. It is quite common in the collegiate world to witness a promiscuous frat boy have a complete 180-degree change once their life has been given to Christ. Not only do their actions change, but so does their view on life, their worldly pursuits, and their personality in some forms even changes. Sometimes people from their old life will run into them, and they will not even recognize them.[48]

There are many other religions that claim to have transformative powers. Buddhism, for example, believes in love and peace and is known to produce positive changes in a person. The difference is that Buddhism tries to perfect the individual through works. They believe that if the person changes, they

[48] Mental recognition, not physical

can work their way to perfection or nirvana.[49] True Christianity does not believe that a person can become perfect or that a person can even become good.[50] Disciples of Christ believe that through Him, they are made clean, and by trying to follow His example, they can become better people.

The key part of transformation is that it is started by God, paid for by Christ's blood, and carried out by the Holy Spirit. No part of transformation is done by a person. Transformation is not about works or faith. We are given faith by God. Faith is not found by any disciple. That is why transformation is so powerful. When we try to change ourselves, we are using our finite resources. But when God tries to change a person, He can easily do it because He is the origin of salvation and the world.

Traditional Christian Ideology

When it comes to the teachings of Christianity, there is a lot of debate about what it teaches.[51] There are those who believe that Christianity is a religion of hate, teaching that the heathen should either convert or die. Sadly, this tactic has been used by some individuals who do not understand the teachings of Christ.[52] Others claim that Christians are cultish, afraid of anyone different, or stuck in the past and afraid of progress. While all these accusations can be true for specific individuals or

---

[49] Harris, Tom. "How Nirvana Works." *HowStuffWorks*, HowStuffWorks, 9 July 2002, science.howstuffworks.com/science-vs-myth/extrasensory-perceptions/nirvana2.htm. Accessed 2 May 2022.

[50] This is goodness from God's perspective, not ours.

[51] Much of which comes from a lack of historical or theological knowledge

[52] Many individuals use the Crusades, the Conquistador conquests, and the Inquisition to back up these claims. The issue is that the Crusades started as a rebuttal to Islamic military aggression, the Conquistadores were mostly greedy, power-hungry soldiers, and the Inquisition was carried out by weak-minded, power hungry clergy.

churches, none of them are true for the Christian ideology. So, if the above beliefs are not correct, what does Christianity teach? Luckily, Scripture answered this question.[53]

God wanted the ideology of Christianity to be so clear that He had it written four different times (Matthew, Mark, Luke, and John). The first time it was written was in the actual law, though it did not contain the second part spelled out. The next three times are the same story written by different disciples. Matthew, Mark, and Luke all record the conversation between Christ and the lawyer because it is the summation of everything God had commanded Israel.[54] All the laws and all the regulations were summed up by these two points. Love God with everything possible, and love everyone possible. There are no stipulations on who to love or how to love. Therefore, no person—no matter their skin pigmentation, orientation, religious conviction, or political beliefs—can be ignored. Christians are called to love, nothing more, nothing less.

This has also been understood for millennia. It is important to remember that Christ was speaking to a Jewish lawyer because it was their job to study every minute detail of the Mosaic law. This means that the Jews understood that God wanted His people to love Him completely and love those around them. Since this is the summary of the law, there are two secondary ideologies that stem from these commands. First, we have *love your neighbor,* and secondly, we have *love your enemies*.

The first, and probably most popular, is *love your neighbor*. The best way to explain this concept is through the Good Samaritan parable. As mentioned above, this is the idea of helping an individual in need. The story shows that the Samaritan had nothing in common with the injured Jew; they were cultural enemies. The Samaritan helps him anyway.

---

[53] Deuteronomy 6:4–5, Matthew 22:37–40, Mark 12:30–31, and Luke 10:27

[54] Luke 10:27, Matthew 22:37–40, and Mark 12:29–31

Samaritans were Jews who had stayed in Israel after the exile. They are called Samaritans because they lived in the northern kingdom of Israel after the split during the reign of the kings and its capital was Samaria.[55] When the exile was over and the Jews returned, the Samaritans had mingled with Gentiles and were considered impure. The Samaritans also had changed their religious practices and theology enough that they were no longer considered Jewish by religion.[56]

The application for this story is simple. Christians are to help anyone, anywhere. That is it. While it may seem like a minor concept, it has had drastic ramifications across history and cultures. The idea of helping someone different was a foreign concept then, and sadly it has become a foreign concept today.

The next minor ideology is *love thy enemy.* If the concept of loving a random individual was radical, loving a personal enemy was even more so. Here God is commanding His people to not only tolerate an enemy's existence but also try and do kind things to and for them. When the body of Christ[57] performs acts of love on those who hate them, they show that love can conquer all. Much of Martin Luther King's civil rights practices were based on this idea. He wanted to love those who hated him and maybe win them over to him and to God.

> Returning hate for hate multiplies hate, adding deeper darkness to a night already devoid of stars. Darkness cannot drive out darkness; only light can

---

[55] 1 Kings 11:31–35

[56] Roat, Alyssa. "The Samaritans: Hope from the History of a Hated People." *Biblestudytools.com*, Salem Web Network, 10 Feb. 2020, www.biblestudytools.com/bible-study/topical-studies/the-samaritans-hope-from-the-history-of-a-hated-people.html. Accessed 2 May 2022.

[57] Another term used for the global church

> do that. Hate cannot drive out hate; only love can do that.[58]

When we show love to those who hate us and to anyone around us in general, we lead people to Christ. The world sees that we act differently, and they want to know why we treat others the way we do, and they want to know how we persevere through the pain and frustration of being treated harshly and not retaliating.

Neo-Gnostic Ideology

When it comes to the ideology of Neo-Gnostics, there has not been a written set of beliefs. Neo-Gnosticism is more of a general set of convictions that most, though not all, progressive Christians believe. The primary idea of Neo-Gnosticism is a rejection of many traditional Christian beliefs. They reject Scripture's teachings on sexuality, on marriage, on the supremacy of Scripture, and on God Himself.

If Neo-Gnosticism was boiled down to a concise statement like traditional Christianity, it would be this" "love yourself, pursue your desires, and truth is unknowable." Some secondary ideologies that can be found in Neo-Gnosticism are *synchronism* and *self-love*.

Synchronism is the idea of combining two concepts by blending them together. In this case, it is adding any belief in addition to Christ. Scripture teaches that Christ is the only way to heaven,[59] but Neo-Gnostics believe that Christ plus something else is fine. Most believe that Christ is an important part of Christianity, but they believe that they need to add certain

---

[58] "Strength to Love Quotes by Martin Luther King Jr." *Goodreads.com*, 2022, www.goodreads.com/work/quotes/50833-strength-to-love. Accessed 2 May 2022.

[59] John 3:16, Acts 4:12, and John 14:5–7h

things to complete the equation. This can be social justice, scientific unity, or scriptural reworking.

Many Neo-Gnostics are fine with the idea that Scripture is not complete or that it has cultural issues that need to be changed. Since Scripture was written long ago, by many authors, in different languages, the argument is that mistranslations occurred, and we are now using an incorrect document.[60] The error in this argument will be discussed in a different section, but for now, it can just be said that this argument is not new, and it is not a strong argument.

Synchronization goes even deeper because Christ becomes secondary to whatever the *other* is. He is never first. If He was first, there would be no synchronization to begin with. Synchronization only occurs when there is a lack of trust in Christ.

The Misconception of Self-Love

Self-love is our second ideology. It within itself is a fascinating ideology. Like most traditional Gnostic beliefs, Neo-Gnostics take a practice and flip it. Therefore, instead of focusing on others, Neo-Gnostics focus on their own desires. The belief is that the self is the most important thing. This means that the self needs to be protected above all.

Those who practice self-love focus on themselves before they help others. Many practitioners do serve others, but there is a difference. Neo-Gnostics have a point at which they will no longer help because it is affecting their mental health. All individuals have a similar point, but the Neo-Gnostic's breaking point can be drastically lower than other charitable ideologies. In some cases, the breaking point has been reduced to zero. This is not an acceptable thing, no matter the ideology.

---

[60] Giles, Keith. "How Your Bible Is Lying to You." *Keith Giles*, 12 July 2021, www.patheos.com/blogs/keithgiles/2021/07/how-your-bible-is-lying-to-you/. Accessed 3 May 2022.

On the outside, the idea of self-love always sounds nice. Self-care can be an important part of staying healthy, but many individuals today take it too far. Self-love and self-care have turned into an overly materialistic practice where individuals seem to care more about their looks, social status, and self-meditation than they do about loving others.

Ending Remarks

Ideology is the foundation of any individual's life. Everything revolves around what they believe because what they believe influences what they do. If a person follows a traditional Christian worldview, they are going to follow the teachings and practices of Christ. They will love their neighbor and their enemy. They will give to the poor and less fortunate. True disciples of Christ have radically changed the world for the better.[61] This is because what a person believes drastically changes their interpretation of an event. Disciples see the world as Christ saw the world, not how the world sees the world.

Everyone has an ideology that they live their life by. The only difference between one person and the next is that some know what they believe, some are still searching, and others hold fast to a belief that they have not consciously meditated on. The first two are understandable; the last is not. It is fine to search for truth. This, in fact, is something everyone should be doing at all times. Once an individual finds the ideology that they believe is the truth, it is their duty to dive as deep into that ideology to make sure that it is just as true at the bottom as it was at the top.

---

[61] Modern science, philosophy, and ethics have all been heavily influenced by Christian beliefs. Also, things such as slavery, child labor, woman's rights, and other forms of equality have all happened because of Christian beliefs.

What is not fine is for an individual to just grab the first ideology presented to them[62] and never investigate it. This leads to mentally weak individuals who have no idea what they believe, and they start to fall for every nice-sounding scheme presented to them. When a foundation is built on a rock, it will stand forever. But when it is built on sand, any small tide will wash it away.[63] When an ideology is built on truth, it will last, but when it is built on fallacies, it will crumble after the first hardship.

62 Whether it be Christianity or any other worldview

63 Matthew 7:24–27

3

Hermeneutics

...the man who has become like God has forgotten how he was at his origin and has made himself his own creator and judge.

—Dietrich Bonhoeffer[1]

The next crossroad we will encounter has fewer splits than the last juncture, but that does not mean that it is any less confusing. One reason for this confusion is that it is a broad topic. Scriptural interpretation[2] delves into many different aspects of Christianity. To make things easier, this topic has been split into two parts. First, we will discuss interpretation itself, and then we will look at theology by itself. This is the second fork because we have to understand how to read Scripture before we can try to see what it teaches. Interpretation is vitally important for biblical understanding. Just like the last fork, there are many paths that can be taken. But all will lead to dead ends and wrong destinations. This is because we have tried to inject Scripture with our own ideas, not God's.

[1] Dietrich, Bonhoeffer. "Ethics."

[2] Which is what *hermeneutics* means

A large issue with modern Neo-Gnostics is that they do not understand Scripture. This can be because of poor personal study, bad pastoral teaching, or a combination of the two. Many of them will claim that they grew up in a Christian household, that they went to church, and that they had a believing faith in God. But if they did not understand Scripture and what it taught, then their faith is one of two things. It is either dormant or non-existent.[3] This is why all disciples need to discuss and understand scriptural interpretation. Having a base understanding of hermeneutics allows believers to combat basic errors and misunderstandings.

Scripture is simple to read when one understands the context and wording. Understanding these two items only requires a minor amount of study. This is why when Guttenberg's printing press allowed the Bible to be made for common, or almost common, distribution, thousands of European families were able to read and understand God's word. They were not theologians, nor did they have an extensive education like modern western countries. What they did have[4] was a thirst for God.

The best way to know God is by reading His very own words to His people. Scripture is the words of God spoken through His prophets.[5] The Bible is simple to read and under-

---

[3] There are many individuals who claim to be believers that have zero habits or beliefs of Christ. This means that many kids grow up in "Christian households" when, in fact, they grew up in religiously superstitious households with mostly secular characteristics. There are also many churches that do not preach God nor the gospel. Therefore, claiming that one grew up in the church as a defense for scriptural understanding is futile. Religious cultures (like the American South) are riddled with churches that follow the more health-and-wealth kind of gospel than Christ's. Lastly, if one does not understand Scripture and believes that they are in fellowship with Christ when they are not, it is easy to see why so many "believers" are starting to fall away.

[4] And what our culture, in many ways, is lacking

[5] There are forty different authors, but one theme. Many different individuals, over centuries in different languages, yet there is one understood story.

stand, but for our purposes, we are going to discuss two important keys to help with its understanding. Before we can continue our journey, we have to talk about the ways we read Scripture. Here we will discuss the concepts of context and inerrancy.

It is important to discuss scriptural interpretation to see what beliefs are needed and which ones are not.[6] If Scripture is proven to contain inaccurate information, then believers need to reevaluate their beliefs.[7] If, on the other hand, scriptural content and beliefs can be defended, then believers can rest more assured in their faith.

The main issue that Neo-Gnostics present is that Scripture, as it is today, is incomplete or wrong. The claim is that a document written in multiple different languages[8] over a few millennia cannot be correct. It is either missing pieces or mistranslated. This belief is the main argument against doctrine or biblical practices that the progressive world now deems untasteful.[9] These untasteful concepts include such things as misogyny, racism, and homophobia. The issue becomes: Does Scripture actually state what Neo-Gnostics claim that it states?

As stated in the last chapter, many of the beliefs of Neo-Gnostics are concept-based. They do not draw their beliefs from a document or a specific person like many religions. Neo-Gnostics take the culture and the world around them and use that as their base. Now that gay rights have become a primary

---

[6] Here the term "needed" is in reference to salvation. Everything written in the Bible is important, but some beliefs are important for salvation, and some are not.

[7] Again, this is where the concept from last chapter becomes relevant. We must reevaluate our understanding of Scripture and the world in light of what God says. Mankind can stretch texts to mean many different things that they do not mean. This is a dangerous thing.

[8] Hebrew, Aramaic, and Greek

[9] These items are rightfully distasteful.

issue culturally, many Neo-Gnostics align their beliefs with that movement and either reinterpret what Scripture says on the subject or completely throw those verses out. Scripture does not say much about homosexuality. But what it does say shows that God is not in favor of the practice itself. Neo-Gnostics focus on the condemnation of the act found in Scripture and try to either explain away the verses or alter them entirely. We will discuss this more thoroughly later. But to reiterate the point another way, Neo-Gnostics use the current culture as a compass and force Scripture to go along with it.[10]

Interpreting Scripture

The first interpretation method we are going to focus on is context. As students learn in literature classes, context is king. Trying to explain a passage in any book without understanding what is happening before is impossible. Explain Frodo throwing the One Ring into Orodruin[11] at the end of *The Return of the King* without reading the first two books. It is not possible, is it? This is why context is vitally important.

Next is factual correctness, otherwise known as lack of error or inerrancy. For Scripture to be believed, it must be inerrant. This means that no part of Scripture has been proven false. If no aspect of Scripture[12] can be shown to be false, then Scripture is inerrant. If it can be proven to be inerrant, then everything in it must be taken seriously. If it can be proven errant, Scripture becomes useless. Anything in error is not worth much. This shows the importance of proving or disproving the Bible. This is why it is called the sword.[13] A sharp sword is a

---

[10] If they do not throw Scripture out completely

[11] Mount Doom; the mountain in Mordor

[12] Historical or scientific

[13] Ephesians 6:17

powerful weapon in combat, but a dull sword is only worth melting down and being used for something else.

Context

The Bible is a complex work of writings, written over fourteen centuries[14] by forty different authors.[15] Because of this, it is common for the basic reader to misunderstand Scripture. It is not that Scripture is difficult or impossible to understand; it is that most people have cultural differences from those found in the Bible, or they do not take the time to study Scripture to see how well it connects with itself. These misunderstandings can be classified in two ways. Most misunderstandings are just simply a lack of knowledge. Most of the people who fall in this category are either new believers or have not developed the discipline of personal study. There are sixty-six books in the Bible, and they range from poetry to history. This range can confuse readers if they do not understand which version they are reading. Obviously, a person would read a poem very differently than how they would read a history text. Shakespeare is read differently than the history of Germany.

The second category is a little more serious. There are some who try to make Scripture say what they want it to say. This is done by either ignoring the context or rewriting the passage. We tend to like things that match our personal opinions. Being correct is a wonderful feeling, especially when we are dealing

---

14 "When Was the Bible Written?" *AllAboutTruth.org*, www.allabouttruth.org/when-was-the-bible-written-faq.htm#:~:text=The%20Bible%20was%20written%20over%20a%20period%20of. Accessed 21 Oct. 2021.

15 "How Many People Wrote the Bible?" *AllAboutTruth.org*, www.allabouttruth.org/how-many-people-wrote-the-bible-faq.htm#:~:text=There%20are%2040%20authors%20of%20the%20books%20of. Accessed 21 Oct. 2021.

with complicated parts of life. Once we have established an opinion on an issue, it is usually easier to ignore countering opinions and facts so that we can keep our decision as it is. People tend to become very attached to their beliefs, no matter how important or trivial it is. Take the idea of cookies. If one person likes chocolate chip and another does not, the chocolate chip person can feel defensive over their opinion on their favorite cookie. It is crazy, but that is how we are.

Because of this, it is easy to see why we want Scripture to match our opinions. The issue is that Scripture is not some small thing that can be rewritten to match current theories. Scripture is a complex document that deals with important aspects of life. It is a finished document that cannot be changed. Unlike the first misunderstanding, this one is a real issue. We cannot ignore aspects of the Bible because we do like them or because we are too lazy to do our research. We also cannot force Scripture to back up our opinions just to make ourselves feel better. Lastly, Scripture, being the word of God, speaks to any situation we will ever face. It has relevance in any aspect of our life. This is one amazing feature of it being God's word.

If we find ourselves misunderstanding something because we have not spent adequate time studying that subject, that is understandable. Everyone lacks knowledge of something. Acknowledging where we need help is always a sign of maturity. Whether it is in understanding the Bible or in some other area in life, it is always good to admit that someone older and wiser can help. But it is a whole different issue to try to change Scripture based off of personal or cultural opinions. There are many beliefs held by the emerging Neo-Gnostics that have absolutely no scriptural backing. These issues can stem from contextual misunderstandings or, even worse, contextual reworking.

Contextual misunderstanding means that an individual takes a verse or passage and believes it says something that it would not say if the entire chapter or book was incorporated. Contextual reworking means that an individual tries to recreate a passage to say what they want it to say. They do this either because they are honestly trying to follow God, and they believe that man has wronged His Scripture. Or they want God's word to match their ideological views. Both are bad, but the second is worse.

Many Neo-Gnostics believe that there are specific commands of God that either do not apply anymore or should not be followed. Most scholars agree that there are some laws that Christians no longer have to follow. But there is a major difference here between traditional scholars and Neo-Gnostics. Scripture does possess some laws that we no longer have to follow, but these laws fall into two specific categories. As for the laws that Neo-Gnostics do not want to follow, most of their objections come from perceived mistranslations of the Hebrew or Greek texts or from cultural objections.

The first set of laws from the Old Testament that believers no longer have to follow are the sacrificial laws. Sacrifice, which is mentioned in the Mosaic Law, is no longer required because Christ was the everlasting sacrifice. Because of this, Christians no longer follow sacrificial laws. The second set is the civil laws. These are the laws pertaining to the Israeli nation. Since they were only meant for the ancient nation of Israel, we no longer have to follow them. Many parts of the Old Testament were meant to point to Christ. In fact, the whole Bible points to Christ. Because of this, there are many practices that would be redundant now that Christ has come, died for our sins, and now sits victorious over Satan and death.

Other laws, such as those against murder, theft, and rape, are classified as moralistic laws. Obviously, these are still pertinent to our lives today. Moralistic laws can be seen in most civil societies throughout most of history. An example of this and how mankind has believed in the same morals since the beginning of writing is the code of Hammurabi.[16] His code is one of

---

[16] History.com Editors. "Code of Hammurabi." *History*, 21 Aug. 2018,

the earliest codes ever written and has many of the same moralistic laws as the Israelites hundreds of years later. The only difference was the severity of the punishment.[17]

When it comes to the perceived mistranslations, most of the issues come from a lack of desire to understand or a complete ignorance of the Hebrew words. The most common example of this is with the word *homosexual*. The word *homosexual* was linguistically birthed in the 1860s by Karl Maria Kertbeny.[18] It was slowly adopted by society, and in 1946, The Revised Standard Version Bible finally incorporated the word in its translation. Again, this Bible was first printed in 1946, about eighty years after the term was coined.[19] This alone shows that believers were not trying to remove same-sex persons from their congregations because they disliked their bedroom habits. They were using a newly formed word[20] to explain an ancient practice.

Part of the Neo-Gnostic argument is that Christians wanted homosexuals out of the church, so they took a part of Scripture that had nothing to do with same-sex relationships and made it say what they wanted it to say. They claim that since this word did not exist in ancient Hebrew or Greek, the authors could not

---

www.history.com/topics/ancient-history/hammurabi.

[17] There is only a difference in some areas. Both laws are harsh, but both laws are also very fair, and both Moses and Hammurabi allow for the belief in innocence and gray area punishments. But the laws given by God to Moses where a drastic step forward for mankind.

[18] Tang, GVGK. "150 Years Ago, the Word 'Homosexual' Was Coined in a Secret Correspondence." Medium, 18 Apr. 2020, medium.com/@gvgktang/150-years-ago-the-word-homosexual-was-coined-in-a-secret-correspondence-1803ff9a79bc.

[19] The Forge Online. "Has "Homosexual" Always Been in the Bible?" *United Methodist Insight*, 14 Oct. 2019, um-insight.net/perspectives/has-%E2%80%9Chomosexual%E2%80%9D-always-been-in-the-bible/. Accessed 4 May 2022.

[20] Though, in some forms, old by that point

have been talking about homosexuality. Using this logic, God does not condemn homosexuality. Neo-Gnostics believe that the verses speak about men innocently sleeping in a woman's bed or pedophilia. God does condemn pedophilia and does call us to live above reproach, but those are different concepts from different verses.

An issue with their argument is that even if this particular word did not exist, the act has existed since antediluvian[21] times. It does not matter if this word existed or not at that time in Scripture. God has shown His distaste for this act in a myriad of ways.[22] The story of Sodom and Gomorrah is a prime example. Besides this story, there are a number of verses[23] that speak about homosexuality, and none of them use this term. But, even without the debated word, these verses are still saying the same thing.

Another example is the Greek word arsenokoites. While the definition of this word has been heavily debated, the more accepted definition is a male engaging in same-gender sexual activity; a sodomite or pederast.[24] This term is used only two times in Scripture. It is used in I Corinthians 6:9 and I Timothy 1:10. Both verses are a list of undesirable actions that Paul is saying Christians should not commit.[25]

---

[21] Before the flood

[22] Another question to be asked is why homosexuality suddenly became offensive to Christians? If homosexuality has been a practiced act for millennia, why would it suddenly be a sin? On top of that, it was common for intellectuals or the political elite to have homosexual relations on top of their heterosexual marriages. The rationale does not stand when it is observed from a historical lense.

[23] Leviticus 20:13, Leviticus 18:22, Romans 1:26–27, and I Timothy 1:10, to name a few

[24] "Strong's Greek: 733. ἀρσενοκοίτης (Arsenokoites) -- a Male Engaging in Same-Gender Sexual Activity." *Biblehub.com,* biblehub.com/greek/733.htm. Accessed 25 Jan. 2022.

[25] These are sins just like any other sin. To be clear, homosexuality is no more

Misinterpreting Philippians 4:13

As we saw from the example before, context is critical when trying to understand what a verse is saying. It is very easy to take a section of Scripture out of context and try to make it say anything desired. But to show that this issue can go a different way, here is another commonly misused verse: Philippians 4:13.[26]

Sadly, contextual issues are not only a problem for Neo-Gnostics. Many Christians, and those in the secular world as well, tend to misuse a lot of verses because they sound good, they make the person feel good, or they believe that the verse promises them an easy life. Being able to do anything through the power of Christ, who is God, sounds unbelievable. But this verse loses a lot of its magic when compared to the verses around it, that is, when it is reinserted into its context.

> I rejoiced in the Lord greatly that now at length you have revived your concern for me. You were indeed concerned for me, but you had no opportunity. Not that I am speaking of being in need, for I have learned in whatever situation I am to be content. I know how to be brought low, and I know how to abound. In any and every circumstance, I have learned the secret of facing plenty and hunger, abundance and need. *I can do all things through him who strengthens me* (Phil. 4:10–13 ESV, emphasis added).

---

a sin than any other sin. God condemns any act on the same level. To God, theft and sexual immorality are both deserving of death because they are in opposition to His character.

[26] I can do all things through Him who strengthens me.

Paul is thanking the Philippian church for supporting him financially and through prayer. When the verse is reinserted into its context, it is clear that Paul is not saying he can do whatever he wants, and Christ will bless him. He is stating that he has learned to completely lean on God for his support. He ends with the famous phrase in verse thirteen, concluding that through God, he can endure any form of hardship. He is saying that he has become fully content in Christ. This is not a good luck incantation, as many people use it, but an acknowledgment that God is there supporting disciples through the good as well as the bad.

The last example of how to understand context is the belief known as the health and wealth gospel. Most verses used for this belief (like the one above) are used completely out of context. Another health and wealth verse is Romans 8:28.[27] A lot of people try to use this verse to give them good luck in their worldly pursuits.

Everyone likes the *"And we know that for those who love God all things work together for good"* part, but too many people ignore the *"called according to his purpose"* part. The second part of this verse reinserts the context. All things work together for good when we are living in and working for God's purpose. This verse relates to John 14:21.[28]

The works being mentioned in Romans are the commands required by Christ in John. When we follow the commands of Christ,[29] our plans will prosper. But if the plans pursued are not on that list, this verse does not apply. This is not to say that God

---

27 "And we know that for those who love God all things work together for good, for those who are called according to his purpose." —Romans 8:28(ESV)

28 "Whoever has my commandments and keeps them, he it is who loves me. And he who loves me will be loved by my Father, and I will love him and manifest myself to him." —John 14:21 (ESV)

29 Love God, love our enemies, love our neighbors, and spread the gospel.

will not prosper in other endeavors, but this verse is not speaking on those.

When we encounter passages that seem confusing or contradictory compared to other passages, we must take a step back and look at the context. The last step to understanding the context of a verse is looking at the book in the Bible itself. Paul focuses on faith and grace, while James focuses on works. This is because their letters were meant for different people struggling with different things. Paul wrote to gentiles or Jews living outside of the Middle East, while James wrote to Jews in Israel. Understanding the teachings of Christ from a paganistic background is very different than discussing Christ from a Judaic background.

These men understood that salvation was by Christ's sacrifice, not by our works. But when they were debating or teaching different groups, they were going to focus more heavily on one key aspect over another. Understanding who a book or letter is written to is key to interpreting these confusing verses.

Many issues have arisen from verses like Ephesians 2:8–9[30] and James 2:26.[31] Some individuals take Paul's words incorrectly and think that they no longer have to do charitable works anymore. They believe that since we do not need works for salvation, we do not need to do them. We do not stop doing charitable works because we have evil intent. We usually stop because our everyday lives slowly consume us, and we no longer have time to help. Taking time to help our fellow man is a sacrifice. It takes away from the things we want to do.

On the other hand, many individuals take James' words too far and think that their works are what saves them. This en-

---

30 "For by grace you have been saved through faith. And this is not your own doing; it is the gift of God, not a result of works, so that no one may boast." —Ephesians 2:8–9 (ESV)

31 "For as the body apart from the spirit is dead, so also faith apart from works is dead." —James 2:26 (ESV)

courages them to work their way into heaven by being good. This does produce more charitable works, but they tend to be done out of duty and not out of love. Neither approach is good. This is why correct scriptural interpretation is necessary. This is also why context is the first and easiest interpretational tool to use. The next tool is Biblical inerrancy.

Inerrant

The second item to be discussed is errancy. It is not possible to follow Scripture if it is found to be full of errors. If any part of Scripture is found to be wrong, the rest cannot be trusted. This is the issue with a document such as the Bible. It is an all-or-nothing kind of ideology.

In plain English, errant means to have issues or to be wrong. Or, as the Merriam-Webster dictionary puts it, fallible.[32] Fallible means liable to be erroneous; capable of making a mistake.[33] Inerrant means free from error.[34] This is an important distinction to be made as we discuss scriptural interpretation.

As Wayne Grudem puts it in his *Systematic Theology*: "The inerrancy of Scripture means that Scripture in the original manuscripts does not affirm anything that is contrary to fact."[35] When we deal with religious text, there can be no gray area. Religious documents must either be fully right or fully wrong; there can be no middle ground.

---

32 "Definition of Errant." *www.merriam-Webster.com*, www.merriam-webster.com/dictionary/errant.

33 "Definition of Fallible." *www.merriam-Webster.com*, www.merriam-webster.com/dictionary/fallible.

34 "Definition of Inerrant." *Merriam-Webster.com*, 2017, www.merriam-webster.com/dictionary/inerrant.

35 Grudem, Wayne A. Making Sense of Series: One of Seven Parts from Grudem's Systematic Theology. Grand Rapids, MI, Zondervan, 1994, p. 91.

Jesus's Teachings on Truth

Many Neo-Gnostics believe that Scripture can be re-edited. This means that some verses are appropriate for the culture of today, while others are old-fashioned or offensive. If they are old-fashioned or offensive, they can be ignored or removed. Neo-Gnostics like verses that deal with love and peace, but they dislike the ones about absolute truth, following God's will, or Christ being the only way to salvation. There are even some who believe that Christ was not God at all, yet they still think that He taught a moral philosophy that they can follow.

It is even common for atheists to admire the teachings of Jesus while still believing that He was not God. The problem with this is that Christ stated plainly that He was God.[36] His proclamations of deity obviously cannot be taken lightly. If He claimed to be God and was not, then all His teachings cannot be trusted.

There are many individuals who casually call Him a holy philosopher, a moral guru, or even just another prophet in a long list of prophets. Many of these individuals like His comments on love, equality, and forgiveness. They put His name next to Martin Luther King Jr., Gandhi, and Mother Teresa.

Then a problem arises when people are shown His statements of deity. Some become very perplexed. This perplexity is because they have not actually read His teachings for themselves. Their lack of knowledge of Jesus's other teachings betrays their ignorance of His teachings in general. Christ's statements of deity put mankind in a very weird position. It really leaves only three options. Jesus can only be a lunatic, a liar, or our Lord.

If He was a lunatic, then He was one of the most authentic lunatics in history. Not only was He able to convince thousands

---

[36] John 8:58

of strangers that He was wise,[37] but He was also able to convince over 100 people, who followed Him everywhere He went, of the same. If Christ were a lunatic, then no sane individual would want to listen to anything He said. This would be the same as going to a mentally deranged, homeless man and quoting the babble that comes out of his mouth. No one would take his words seriously.

If Jesus were a liar, then obviously He could not be trusted in anything he said. The world would have seen through His lies when He was on earth, and we would see through His lies now. Christianity has gone through a lot of scrutiny over the two-thousand years it has been around. There have been a lot of intelligent individuals who have tried to refute Christ's teachings and the Bible in general. These investigations always fail or fall short. If Christ lied, His lies would have been exposed a long time ago.

Also, no one would let themselves be crucified over a lie. Jesus was given a lot of chances to recant His statements of godhood. The Jewish elites gave Him a chance, and Pontius Pilate gave Him a chance to recant. But He believed that He was God. This leaves only the last option.

Christ made it very clear that He was God.[38] Everyone around Him knew what He meant when He made these claims. They were specific and only used by God Himself. In John 8:58, Christ uses the phrase "I Am." In English, this does not mean

---

[37] Both in ancient times as well as today

[38] "My Father, who has given them to me, is greater than all, and no one is able to snatch them out of the Father's hand. I and the Father are one." —John 10:29–30 (ESV)

"that they may all be one, just as you, Father, are in me, and I in you, that they also may be in us, so that the world may believe that you have sent me." —John 17:21 (ESV)

"Jesus said to them, 'Truly, truly, I say to you, before Abraham was, I am.'" —John 8:58 (ESV)

very much. But in Hebrew, this was the utterance of God's holy name. The term "I Am" in Hebrew is Yahweh, which is the holiest name for God. The Jews would have understood this connection because of Moses's words in Exodus.[39]

In these verses, Christ Himself clearly claims to be God. Here we have verbal confirmation of Jesus' divinity.[40] Based on these verses, it is no longer possible to claim that Christ did not proclaim to be God. Based on Scripture, Jesus was Lord. Also, it is not possible to claim that He was only a good or moralistic teacher because most of His teachings were based on the idea that He was God. It is impossible to agree with the teachings of Christ without believing that He is God.

Some try to argue that just because He claimed He was God did not mean that those around Him did. Based on Scripture, this is partly correct but mostly incorrect. Those who followed Christ believed that He was God,[41] but those who did not like Him claimed He was from the devil.[42]

When Jesus asked His disciples outright who they thought He was, there was no discussion nor any hesitation. They knew that He was God.[43] But were they the only ones who believed Him to be God? No, a popular story consisting of a Roman cen-

---

[39] "Then Moses said to God, 'If I come to the people of Israel and say to them, "The God of your fathers has sent me to you," and they ask me, "What is his name?" what shall I say to them?' God said to Moses, 'I AM WHO I AM.' And he said, 'Say this to the people of Israel: 'I AM has sent me to you.''" —Exodus 3:13–14 (ESV)

[40] And a clear hint for the trinity

[41] Mark 8:29, Matthew 16:16, and Luke 9:20

[42] Matthew 12:24

[43] "He said to them, 'But who do you say that I am?' Simon Peter replied, 'You are the Christ, the Son of the living God.' And Jesus answered him, 'Blessed are you, Simon Bar-Jonah! For flesh and blood has not revealed this to you, but my Father who is in heaven." —Matthew 16:15–17 (ESV)

turion[44] is a good example that even the pagans knew Christ had power no one else had.[45]

While the centurion never said that He was God, his ending statement shows that he understood Him to be Lord over death. Christ states that no such faith had been found in Israel. This centurion understood the power and authority Christ wielded better than the people of God. But there were still those who did not believe that He was God.

The Pharisees and Sadducees did not believe, at least most of them did not, and the Roman officials did not believe. But as far as Scripture goes, we are not sure if their anger toward Christ was unbelief or disbelief. *Unbelief* means they did not believe who He was; *disbelief* means they did not want to know who He was.[46]

Christ broke their sacred laws and removed the perception of holiness that they had created. Between His deepening of the

---

[44] High Roman military leader

[45] "Now a centurion had a servant who was sick and at the point of death, who was highly valued by him. When the centurion heard about Jesus, he sent to him elders of the Jews, asking him to come and heal his servant. And when they came to Jesus, they pleaded with him earnestly, saying, 'He is worthy to have you do this for him, for he loves our nation, and he is the one who built us our synagogue.' And Jesus went with them. When he was not far from the house, the centurion sent friends, saying to him, 'Lord, do not trouble yourself, for I am not worthy to have you come under my roof. Therefore I did not presume to come to you. But say the word, and let my servant be healed. For I too am a man set under authority, with soldiers under me: and I say to one, "Go," and he goes; and to another, "Come," and he comes; and to my servant, "Do this," and he does it.' When Jesus heard these things, he marveled at him, and turning to the crowd that followed him, said, 'I tell you, not even in Israel have I found such faith.' And when those who had been sent returned to the house, they found the servant well." —Luke 7:2–10 (ESV)

[46] It is hard to say if the pharisees did not believe because of religious pride or because of actual disbelief. Religious pride can be a deadly thing. Too much knowledge can corrupt just as surely as too little.

law and His sacrilegious statements, they desired to kill Him. He was destroying the self-righteous works-based interpretation of Scripture that they had created. It is ironic that those who had dedicated their lives to Scripture and who were the ones looking out for Christ were the ones who missed Him.

Inspired by God

A point that was not mentioned at the beginning but needs to be mentioned now is that Scripture was inspired by God. This means that while men wrote the words in their own language and style, God was there with them. This is similar to how a ghostwriter and an author work. A ghostwriter writes the book, but an author makes sure that nothing incorrect is included.

Therefore, if Scripture is inspired by God, and God is unable to lie,[47] then Scripture must be fully true. Either Scripture is true, or God is able to lie. If Scripture is erroneous, then God can err. If God can err, He is not perfect. If He is not perfect, then He is not worthy of worship. Why worship an imperfect god?

The authors of Titus and Hebrews both state that it is impossible for God to lie. Either God can lie, making Him imperfect and Scripture worthless, or He cannot lie, being an impossibility for Him, and Scripture is inerrant. Again, there cannot be any compromise; we must believe all of Scripture or none of it. We cannot remove the "offensive" parts and keep the rest.

Unfortunately, Christians are forced to use a form of logic called circular reasoning. This is when an argument uses itself to prove itself.[48] If thing 1 is true because of thing 2, and thing 2

---

[47] Titus 1:2 and Hebrews 6:17–18

[48] "Circular Reasoning." *Logicallyfallacious.com,* 2013, www.logicallyfallacious.com/logicalfallacies/Circular-Reasoning. Accessed 4 May 2022.

is only true because of thing 1, then we have circular reasoning. If Scripture is perfect because it is inspired by God, but God is only perfect because of Scripture, we have circular reasoning. The issue is that when it comes to God, Scripture is the only source that discusses His character. We do learn some facts about God through natural revelation.[49] Therefore, Scripture is the only source from which we learn about His character and His promises to us.

This leaves us with earthly verification. When other parts of Scripture are proven to be correct, then the unverifiable parts can be defended. We cannot prove Jesus was God, but if we can prove that He existed, then we gain confidence that what Scripture says about Him is also true. One quick source to prove that Jesus existed is Tacitus, who was one of the greatest Roman historians of Jesus's time.[50] In one of his histories, he mentions Christians being named after a man who was crucified, who they called Christus. The more examples like this we can find to support facts in the Bible, the more likely the spiritual parts are real. This means as science, history, and archeology reveal the authenticity of Scripture, they are also authenticating God. This is why proving the inerrancy of Scripture is important.

An individual cannot claim to follow God while also claiming Scripture to be wrong. Claiming that Scripture is wrong is claiming that God is wrong. One cannot be wrong without the other also being wrong. In this case, God and Scripture are in-

---

[49] This means that through nature, we can see that there is a God. We can also glean some characteristics from nature like His desires for order, justice, love, and that He is the ultimate author and sustainer. The problem is that natural revelation tells us very little about what God has done and any deeper concepts. Natural revelation tells us that there is a God, but it tells us nothing about Jesus.

[50] bethinking.org. "Ancient Evidence for Jesus from Non-Christian Sources." *Bethinking.org*, 9 Feb. 2010, www.bethinking.org/jesus/ancient-evidence-for-jesus-from-non-christian-sources. Accessed 4 May 2022.

tertwined. God and His Word either must be trusted, or the whole thing must be thrown away.

Personal "Special" Revelation

There are many Neo-Gnostics who try to claim to be disciples while throwing the majority of Scripture away. They do this because they believe that they have a special relationship with God that allows them to cast aside Scripture. This is a belief straight from the Gnostics themselves.

Usually when an individual claims to have a special insight into Scripture, they are trying to prove something that Scripture speaks against. Or they are trying to avoid doing something that Scripture says to do. There are those who would claim that they do not need to go to church because they have a special relationship with God. This can mean that God speaks to them (though this is rare) or that they have a general feeling that God is fine with their behavior.

Part of their excuse is that the church is judgmental or is not doing what the Lord wants anyway. They do have a point about judgmental churches. Sadly, there are a lot of prideful churches in the world. Many of them are not conducting the call made by Christ, yet they feel like they can tell everyone else what to do. This is a sad reality in Christendom, but it does not excuse believers from gathering.

Scripture is clear that we are to be in community with other Christians.[51] It does not specify any requirements that the community needs to fulfill. We are to gather and fellowship together. Proverbs 27:17[52] says quite clearly that we need to be in community for mutual growth. For a file to sharpen steel, it has to be in direct connection with it. For Christians to become

---

[51] Hebrews 10:24–25 and Ecclesiastes 4:9–10

[52] "Iron sharpens iron, and one man sharpens another."

sharper in the word of God, we need to be in direct connection with other believers.

God will never give special revelation to an individual that is contrary to His Word. This means that those who claim to have a direct connection to God are using their holy prophetic abilities for self-gain and sloth.

The only times God speaks directly to a person are for prophetic or Scripture-making purposes. God spoke to the men and women in Scripture for very specific purposes. He spoke to Abraham to create His covenants that would bind Himself and the nation of Israel.[53] He spoke to the prophets to condemn Israel for her misdeeds and to point to the savior.[54] And He spoke to Paul to make him His disciple.[55] Each of these examples had a very specific purpose. No one can say that they speak with God and say He is excusing them from His commands. It is a creative excuse, but only that.

Though, there are many individuals who claim to have spoken to Christ right before meeting someone who shared the gospel. This means that God is still speaking to His chosen, but again, only for salvation purposes. There has never been a proven moment when God spoke and allowed a random person to cast aside His word.

Incorrect Revelations about God

To be clear, there have been times in history when theological reformation was required. Martin Luther is a great example of this. He challenged the Roman Catholic Church on doctrine that was unbiblical. He wrote a list of items he did not think the Bible supported and why. But there is a big difference between

---

[53] Genesis 17

[54] Any of the major or minor prophets

[55] Acts 9:1–19

how Luther reformed the church and the Neo-Gnostics' attempt. Luther was humble in his approach and had no desire to split the church. His only desire was for the church to look at his thesis and discuss it. He humbly wanted to make the church better and closure to God. That is not the desire of most Neo-Gnostics. Luther once stated that if the church, through Scripture, could produce a counter-argument to his, he would repent and forsake his ideas.[56] This humility shows that his desire was not to get away with some type of action but to truly discover what God desires.

Most scriptural "revelations" are incorrect revisions trying to excuse a sin or opinion. A good example is the reinterpretation of the Garden of Eden. In a Gnostic and Neo-Gnostic reinterpretation of this story, God becomes evil, and the serpent becomes good. The Tree of Knowledge becomes a symbol of repression instead of a symbol of trusting God.[57]

In this retelling, God's reasoning for keeping the tree from Adam and Eve was because He was afraid of them. He knew that if they ate the fruit, they would become powerful, and this scared Him. The serpent was the true savior because he released them from their state of ignorance. In ancient Gnostic theology, knowledge was the true savior, not Christ. When an individual awoke from their ignorance, they became holy.[58] A

---

[56] Mark, Joshua J. "Luther's Speech at the Diet of Worms." *World History Encyclopedia*, World History Encyclopedia, 9 Dec. 2021, www.worldhistory.org/article/1900/luthers-speech-at-the-diet-of-worms/. Accessed 4 May 2022.

[57] Rudolph, Kurt, and R Mcl Wilson. *Gnosis : The Nature and History of Gnosticism*. San Francisco, Harper & Row, 1987.

[58] This is very similar to the concept of being "woke." Obviously, the idea of awaking to true knowledge as the savior to oppression is a very old idea. Gnosticism might have reached its zenith during the early church years, but its ideas has been around long before that. This shows that awaking to new revelations is a constant in human history. This also shows that the modern progressive Christian is just another reiteration of this ancient

similar concept has grown in Neo-Gnostic theology. Since they believe that truth is subjective and that reality is always changing, knowledge is also always growing. What God commanded as evil at one time now has become good because mankind has spiritually evolved.

This concept is just as wrong today as it was two thousand years ago. As stated before, Neo-Gnostics are re-birthing old theology. The church has encountered these beliefs before and has weighed their worth. Not one of these beliefs has ever held water. They become weak and old, and they always come up wanting.

God created the Tree of Knowledge to show that there was an option. To show that they had free will, there had to be something to choose. Mankind could choose themselves by choosing the tree, or they could choose God by staying away from it. Scripture claims that God is all-powerful, all-knowing, and ever-present. He is truth and wisdom; therefore, He desired for Adam and Eve to rely on Him. He wanted them to follow Him because they loved and trusted Him. Just like an earthly father desires for his children to follow his rules because they believe that he knows best, God desires the same.[59]

When we rely on God, we receive the ultimate understanding of good and evil. We are connected to the origin of everything. When we seek good and evil on our own, we are replacing God as that origin and inserting ourselves. We become the origin of creation, good, and evil. But we are imperfect, finite beings. We can never know what truly is good or evil. Our understanding is constantly changing.

---

practice.

59 There is a belief that the Tree of Knowledge was just that, a normal tree. The only thing that made this tree special was that God said it had purpose. The knowledge of good and evil only occurred because Adam and Eve chose to take their own path, not God's. This belief relies less on the powers of a tree, and more on the separation of man's plan from God's.

The quote at the beginning of this chapter explains this well.

> "...the man who has become like God has forgotten how he was at his origin and has made himself his own creator and judge." —Dietrich Bonhoeffer

When an individual removes God from the center and replaces it with himself, he forgets who or what he is. God is creator and sustainer. When we try to make ourselves the judge and molder of the world, we fail. We fail because we have limited knowledge and wisdom. When an individual encounters something new, they have no experience to rely on. They must, in essence, make it up as they go. This is not a wise practice when it comes to life.

This is why the corruption of the garden was so significant. Not only did Adam and Eve disobey God's commandment, but they also replaced God with themselves. The gravitational force of God that was supposed to exist in our heart or our core was removed from this center, leaving a black hole. This hole now sucks anything it can, destroying everything it comes into contact with.

Special revelation removes God from the center and replaces it with knowledge. But knowledge without God is fake. This is why Neo-Gnostics seem to always be searching. They have not found that one piece of knowledge that will satisfy them. They do not even know what they are in search of. They only know that they are not complete. This is because true satisfaction was thrown away when God was rejected. God is the only thing that will satisfy and fill that void. God has revealed Himself completely in His word; read it and discover the savior.

Ending Remarks

Literature is pointless when read out of context. Verses in Scripture can be made to mean anything that the individual desires when taken away from the whole of the book. Therefore Scripture, or any book really, needs to be read carefully and with the whole context in mind. This is no easy task. To understand context, we really need to just sit down and continually read all of the Bible. Reading other books can be very beneficial, but when it comes to context, reading the Bible itself is what matters.

Sadly, some things have no easy avenue. Studying Scripture is very rewarding, and if made a habit, it can radically change one's life. Dietrich Bonhoeffer said that reading Scripture was a duty; it just required one step after another. If this duty is performed, God will reward us. It may not be an earthly reward,[60] but God will reward His people.

Another aspect of biblical study is the investigation into the inerrancy of Scripture. Every Christian should take some time and continually study. There are countless books demonstrating the proof of Scripture. There are histories, theologies, and Bible study curricula. Picking the right book to help is by itself a daunting task. Finding credible sources takes time. But this is also a valuable skill to develop.

But add on top of that actually reading and studying Scripture, and this can feel incredibly difficult. Understanding the historical and archaeological proofs of Scripture can also make one's faith stronger. If there is no proof for Christianity, then it is a dead faith, and we need to move on. But if there is proof, Christianity can be taken seriously.

Those who engage in this type of study are participating in apologetics.[61] Studying how to defend anything leads to a

[60] Though peace and contentment tend to be rewards.

[61] The study of the defense for a religion

stronger faith or understanding in that thing. So, studying apologetics will lead to a stronger faith. This is because the student learns how little Scripture has changed over the last one to two thousand years. Scripture also mentions historical events and cities, and as we learn about these facts in textbooks, we see that Scripture is real and alive.

Scripture Inspired by God

God is the inspiration for Scripture. This means that He guided and prompted the authors on what to write. They wrote it in their language and style, but He is the underlying thread in what they wrote. This also means that if Scripture is wrong, then God is wrong.

When individuals try to remove sections out of Scripture, they are doing this because they believe some parts of Scripture are not culturally appropriate. Neo-Gnostics have become comfortable with their sin, and they do not like it when Scripture condemns their actions. If God is incorrect on some things, He cannot be trusted on anything. If Scripture and God are wrong, then all of Christianity is wrong, and it should fade away with the other forgotten religions.

Scripture is the only inspired word of God. No other document or authority has the stamp of God. This is why when Neo-Gnostics claim they have a special relationship with God, they are nullifying Scripture and are acting outside of God's will. God has spoken to individuals before. Every reference to holy communication in Scripture has a specific point. No revelation has ever been given by God that has nullified any previous command. Even when He came down Himself, He did not nullify His word. The parts that we no longer follow have been fulfilled by Him. Christ is the only person who has the authority to fulfill anything in Scripture. No person can claim to have a special relationship or revelation from God that enables them to ignore God's word.

Scripture is the holy word of God. If it is wrong, then everything Christians believe is wrong, and everything built on Christianity is wrong. This is not a simple battle over semantics. This is a battle over truth. That is why this is the second post on the narrow path. If our understanding of hermeneutics is wrong, then we have been heading down the wrong path for the last two millennia. This path has led to lies and despair. If Scripture is wrong, and God along with it, then we have all been fooled. We have to be absolutely sure that what we teach, read, and believe is true. Life and truth rest on it.

4

Theology

God is most glorified in us when we are most satisfied in Him.

—John Piper[1]

We have now moved on to the next stop. Unlike the last two stops, this one does not have many paths leading off of it. Once we know how to read Scripture, it is a lot easier to understand the teachings it has. The branches off of this path deal with denominations and the differences they deal with.

While the last chapter dealt with the idea of scriptural interpretation, this chapter will deal with scriptural doctrine. Once an individual comes to grips with context, they can begin to delve into the theological realm. In reality, these are done simultaneously, but for our purposes, they have been broken down into two sections.[2]

---

[1] Piper, John. "God Is Most Glorified in Us When We Are Most Satisfied in Him." *Desiring God*, www.desiringgod.org/messages/god-is-most-glorified-in-us-when-we-are-most-satisfied-in-him. Accessed 8 May 2022.

[2] Hermeneutics and theology

This chapter is going to try to sum up the theology of both Neo-Gnostics and traditional Christianity. This in itself is no small feat. Out of the two, traditional Christianity will be much simpler to explain. This is because there is a specific book that explains in quite a bit of detail what they believe. There is also two-thousand years' worth of documentation and debate over the values and theology of this faith. Thousands of minds have worked out the teachings of Scripture,[3] and this has created a solid path to traverse when viewing theology.

Neo-Gnosticism, on the other hand, will be a tricky belief system to explain. This is because it, as said before, does not draw from a specific document or deity. This makes it difficult to summarize. On top of that, it is a constantly changing ideology. What was condemned last year is embraced today. What was embraced yesterday is forbidden tomorrow. Also, there are no official theologians or scholars. This ever-changing set of beliefs tends to confuse those outside the fold, and it has also confused many within. Again, it is hoped to discuss all beliefs in their strongest case, not their weakest. The issue is that some arguments are based on the concept of fairness and love, not on actual facts, reality, or truth. This foundation has added its own form of difficulty. But nonetheless, an attempt will be made to display Neo-Gnostic beliefs honestly.

---

[3] Though there are many different concepts when it comes to certain doctrine, there remains one single pillar that all true believers look to. This pillar is Christ and His work on the cross. Denominations may differ on baptism, creation, or sanctification, but no one argues about Christ. Those that do are not Christians; they may be approaching salvation, but they have not arrived yet. Christ is the foundation of this faith, and this is the only thing that cannot be debated without truly compromising one's faith.

Neo-Gnostic Doctrine

When it comes to Neo-Gnosticism, doctrine becomes very loose. The easiest way to sum up the current Neo-Gnostic situation is by looking at the current western culture. The modern culture has fully embraced an idea called post-modernism. The Encyclopedia Britannica defines post-modernism as: "a late 20th-century movement characterized by broad skepticism, subjectivism, or relativism; a general suspicion of reason; and an acute sensitivity to the role of ideology in asserting and maintaining political and economic power."[4] To quickly summarize this definition, we can say that post-modernists dislike ideology, and they try to deconstruct everything. As we discussed in chapter one, everyone has an ideology. This puts Neo-Gnostics in an interesting position. Since they follow post-modernist thought, they tend to dislike any ideology but their own. This is because they do not see their beliefs as an ideology. They believe that they are practicing an anti-ideology: the ideology that will end ideologies and bring mankind into a form of earthly utopia.[5]

Post-modernists tend to deconstruct everything around them.[6] They see the evil, hypocrisy, and avarice in every organization or institution. While this is not different from their parents' generations, they do not look over the ills. Past generations have looked at the same issues and decided that the

---

[4] Duignan, Brian. "Postmodernism | Definition, Doctrines, & Facts." *Encyclopædia Britannica*, 25 Oct. 2018, www.britannica.com/topic/postmodernism-philosophy.

[5] There have been many comparisons to books like *Brave New World, 1984,* and *The Giver*. These books tell stories in different types of dystopian or utopian variations of our own. In all three, the government has gained complete control of society and have pacified the citizens through different means. The issue is that life in these books compared to the current Western world is a shell. We possess many freedoms, luxuries, and commodities that individuals in these stories can only dream of.

[6] Whether that be religion, economics, or politics

good these groups did outweigh the bad (or maybe the bad was not as bad as it is now, it is hard to say). Modern Neo-Gnostics do not. They believe that they can cure the world with a hot knife, slicing away all the sins by removing all groups or ideas that they believe are contributing. The big problem is that after they deconstruct, they tend not to reconstruct. This is the opposite of what we talked about before. Deconstruction is not necessarily a bad thing, but if it is not followed by studious reconstruction, it is very damaging. Neo-Gnostics also cut away everything until the institution that they are attacking has nothing left. This holy savagery does not allow for a group to reconstruct.

When it comes to the Neo-Gnostic specifically, they are very critical of traditional Christianity, Scripture, and the church in general. Traditional Christianity is one of the largest institutions in the Western world. It is the oldest[7] and has the most pull over society.[8] America is still technically classified as a Christian nation,[9] and there are a lot of people who think that they know what Christianity teaches and what Scripture says. But in almost every situation, when they are questioned, they tend to reveal their ignorance. Not only are many Neo-Gnostics ignorant of Christian history and the Bible, but they are also very confident in their knowledge of those things. This combination has led to a lot of interesting theological combinations.

Some of the beliefs that are found in almost every Neo-Gnostic[10] are subjective truth, cultural superiority, and acceptance. Subjective truth refers to the idea that truth cannot be

---

[7] Dating back to the first century

[8] Most individuals are associated with the church in some way. While this is fading in countries like the United States, places like the southern states are still heavily influenced by the church in some capacity.

[9] Though that can be heavily contested

[10] And in every progressive post-modern individual

truly discovered. Truth is relative compared to a person, society, or culture. Cultural superiority means that the current culture that Neo-Gnostics live in defeats any statements from a previous culture. This is how they defeat arguments raised by Christians on areas of sin. They claim that those issues were only called bad because the culture said so, not because God did. They got it wrong back then; we have it right this time. That is their argument. Lastly, acceptance is the idea that we are required to accept every aspect of a person's life to show them love.

Neo-Gnosticism and Subjective Truth

Subjective truth is the first belief of a Neo-Gnostic. The concept of truth will be more thoroughly dealt with in a different chapter. But for now, we can say that Neo-Gnostics believe that truth is subjected to the individual. This means that everything one person believes can be fully true, and what another person believes can be fully true. These beliefs can be fully opposed, but in the world of subjective truth, that does not matter.

A sibling belief of subjective truth is a lack of absolutes. Just like with subjective truth, this belief follows the idea that no belief can be proven correct absolutely. If nothing can truly be proven, then everything can be on the table. So again, what one person believes can be just as true as what another person believes, even if they contradict each other.

These two beliefs allow Neo-Gnostics to believe that all religious roads lead to heaven.[11] They believe that God does not punish people for worshiping the wrong religion because all religions are equal. If truth is relative, then who are we to deny the journey that someone else is traveling? Their journey is between them and God.[12]

---

[11] Or whatever afterlife destination the individual believes in

[12] Ironically, this is a Christian concept; the only difference is that Neo-

Accepting All Lifestyles

If there is no such thing as absolute truth or absolutes in general, we need to be accepting of everything and everyone. This belief is very similar to Christ's commands to love one's neighbor, but there is a small twist. Neo-Gnostics believe that since we cannot prove anything, we cannot judge anyone's lifestyle. This means that we need to accept everyone's identification, no matter what it is.

This belief can be a little confusing at first because of the base terminology. Neo-Gnostics use multiple words to mean the same thing. They will use the words *love, acceptance,* and *tolerance.* While they use multiple words, they really just mean one, acceptance.

The definition of love[13] is to care for someone or something greatly. Acceptance[14] means not having any issues with a thing, and tolerance[15] means allowing something to be, though that thing may be different. When Neo-Gnostics explain what they mean by love, they describe "allowing someone to do something that they believe will make them happy." This is where the idea of "you do you" comes from. The idea is that to be loving, we need to let other people do whatever they want. Even if that lifestyle hurts themselves or others, it does not matter. They believe that it only matters to let people be who they want to be.

When they use the word *love,* what they mean is acceptance. They believe that all things should be accepted. All sexual orientations should be accepted, all gender expressions

---

Gnostics use that concept to excuse sinful actions while Christians use it to explain sanctification.

[13] Unselfish loyal and benevolent concern for the good of another

[14] Capable or worthy of being accepted

[15] Sympathy or indulgence for beliefs or practices differing from or conflicting with one's own

should be accepted, and many other social expressions should be accepted. Since all paths lead to God, why does it matter how they identify or express themselves?

One big part of acceptance is the belief that society or religion should not require specific qualifications to fit in. They believe that a loving God would not force His followers to behave in a specific way to be with Him. Again, this relates to the belief in subjective truth. If truth is subjective, so is the path to God.

This belief is slightly perplexing. It is perplexing because all of nature has laws. This is why we study science. Everything in nature has a rational, explainable law that it follows. There are rare examples of species that break these laws, but they still fit into the fabric of nature.

There are requirements to even be considered alive. There are other examples, such as oxygen, which is required to breathe. Food is required for energy, and every biome has specific requirements for animals to survive there.

A polar bear could never live in the Sahara, while a camel cannot live in the arctic. Any rational person can understand why. The camel is not made to live in the bitter cold, and the polar bear is not designed to live in the scorching heat. Every animal lives in the biome that it is meant to live.

If science has requirements, why should civil society lack requirements? Societal requirements, also known as laws, are needed so that everyone acts in the best interest of those around them. A lawless society breaks down into chaos, and pain or destruction occurs.

Beliefs Based on Culture

Neo-Gnostics derive their final beliefs not from Scripture but from culture. They believe that mankind is slowly being perfected. This belief comes from evolution. If evolution is correct, then everything in existence is going from a state of chaos to a state of order. This evolutionary process is coupled with the belief that man is naturally good. The combination of these two beliefs means that as mankind has developed their societies, they have gone from unjust to just. Neo-Gnostics believe that continual progress is required for mankind to finally reach the achievable pinnacle of morality and justice. Since mankind is naturally good, it is up to those who have been enlightened, or freed from social constraints, to pave the path to enlightenment. The translation of all of this is that the modern culture is holier than more ancient cultures.

So, if Scripture has passages that claim that acts or lifestyles like homosexuality, fornication, or adultery are wrong, it is because the original culture was repressive. God would not repress his creation like that. Neo-Gnostics also go a step further and claim that Scripture should align with the culture, not the other way around. Many years ago, a man named Nietzsche wrote extensively on how Christian morals were a degradation of society that needed to be eradicated for the "overman" to take control. He believed, and his teachings have become popular,[16] that Christian morals were a drag on society. He thought that they made mankind weak, and he desired for them to be removed.

Neo-Gnostics believe a very similar thing. They believe that the absolute truths taught by Christ and Scripture are expressions of an ancient society and should be updated. Unlike Nietzsche, they believe that these laws do not come from God but from society. If modern society is better than ancient society, then certain undesirable aspects of Scripture should be changed to reflect the more accepting modern society.

They believe that we know better now, and because of this, we should alter Scripture. They also claim that when Scripture was being written, they did not have to deal with certain lifestyles like we do today. Since they did not have to deal with them, they made unaccepting rules. Now that we understand

---

[16] Even if they do not know who he is or what he actually taught

these lifestyles more accurately, we can make more accurate rules.

Summarizing Neo-Gnosticism

These are the most important teachings of Neo-Gnosticism. Again, it is hard to summarize a belief system that does not draw from a specific source. Of if they do follow a source, it is one that is ever-changing. Neo-Gnostics do follow the flow of the modern Western culture, which shifts and changes as time goes by. Because of this constant change, it is difficult to pinpoint the exact beliefs of this group.[17] Also, like any group, not all Neo-Gnostics agree with each other. But this list hopes to argue for the central beliefs that are held by the most Neo-Gnostics.

Primary Doctrine for Traditional Christianity

It is time to discuss the main beliefs of traditional Christianity. These are not all the beliefs held by disciples of Christ but the most important beliefs. This first section will lay out the primary doctrines. Primary theologies are those that deal with Christ. When theologies deal with Christ, we must agree with what Scripture says. Primary doctrine is that which deals with the life, character, and purpose of Christ and God. When we hold a different opinion than what Scripture speaks on, we are not worshiping the Christian God.

This is a key issue that Neo-Gnostics have against traditional Christianity. They believe that one must follow a myriad

[17] Calling them a group is even difficult. Their adherence to the progressive belief system is extremely varied. Just like their ancient Gnostic counterparts, classifying them under one umbrella is more based on loose allegiance than on actual concrete membership.

of rules to be saved. This is not true. To be saved, there is only one requirement, and that is to believe in Christ.[18]

The man who hung next to Jesus was saved only because he believed that Christ was lord.[19] It is clear here and through other passages[20] that salvation only comes through belief in Christ. This does bring up two important questions. Primarily, if salvation comes through faith in Christ alone, what is the purpose of discussing theology? On top of that, why separate some doctrine from others?

This is done for two reasons. The first reason to write on theology is to understand who Christ is. If we have a wrong impression of Christ, we cannot be saved because we will be worshiping a fake Christ. In essence, this is idolatry.[21] It was easier for the crucified thief because he saw the incarnate Christ. He hung next to Him and heard His actual words. Unfortunately, we do not get that amazing luxury. We have the stories, the writings, and the witnesses, but we will never see Him in person until He comes again or we go to Him after death.[22]

The second reason is purely for mankind. We learn about God from Scripture, and we must organize the Bible in a way

---

[18] "One of the criminals who were hanged railed at him, saying, 'Are you not the Christ? Save yourself and us!' But the other rebuked him, saying, 'Do you not fear God, since you are under the same sentence of condemnation? And we indeed justly, for we are receiving the due reward of our deeds; but this man has done nothing wrong.' And he said, 'Jesus, remember me when you come into your kingdom.' And he said to him, 'Truly, I say to you, today you will be with me in paradise.'" —Luke 23:39–43 (ESV)

[19] Luke 23:39–43

[20] Acts 14:12, John 14:6, Ephesians 2:8–9, John 3:16–18, and Romans 10:9–10

[21] Worshipping something other than God

[22] Unless you are one of the few individuals who has had Christ visit in a dream for gospel purposes. Those individuals are few and have received an amazing blessing.

that our simple, finite minds can comprehend. Thus, we need to look at theology as primary or secondary. All Scripture is important, but some are more important than others.[23]

Inside Theology

It is always a good thing to investigate theology. Investigation keeps the mind and spirit sharp and vigilant. This is why the church conducts Bible studies and the like. The problem is that a lot of Christians no longer want to discuss theology. Instead, they just want to participate in the surface-level practices[24] and then go back to their secular lives during the week. To make things worse, individuals want to only surround themselves with like-minded people, which leads to stagnation. Paul wrote to Timothy:

> For the time is coming when people will not endure sound teaching, but having itching ears they will accumulate for themselves teachers to suit their own passions, and will turn away from listening to the truth and wander off into myths. (2 Tim. 4:3–4 ESV)

Paul knew well that this religious isolation would become a prominent force. It had obviously already started in his day. Therefore, this is not the first time it has happened, and it will not be the last. The discussion on theology must occur, or heresies will creep into the church. Pastors will start preaching

---

[23] Again, this is only so that we can comprehend a perfect, infinite God. We cannot understand things unless they have been boxed up, compartmentalized, and sorted by a hierarchy. While this is unfortunate, it is the reality and we cannot fight against it. We can only find ways to explain it.

[24] Like attending church on Sunday and Wednesday

health and wealth or Neo-Gnostic theology, and those only lead to despair.

All Scripture is important, and all the laws and requirements within it are important. But some beliefs are necessary for salvation, and some are not. Beliefs that are argued over and disagreed on are secondary beliefs. Since we can debate secondary theologies without endangering our faith, they can be used as fun mental exercises. It is good for believers to debate with each other. This is the form of faith sharpening that Scripture speaks about. A more playful name for secondary theologies is "coffee shop doctrine."[25] A few popular examples are new earth vs. old earth and pre-, post-, and mid-tribulation. While they are important to discuss, they do not pertain to salvation. We cannot treat secondary theologies the same way that we treat primary ones. They are completely different, and they need to be discussed as such.

What the Christian Faith Is About

There are many versions of how to summarize the Christian faith. Every denomination has some way to summarize what they believe in a quick, concise way. One of the best ones, and the one used here, is the Nicene Creed. The theologians that made this creed stated the most important beliefs (minus salvation by faith) as concisely as possible. It goes as thus:

> I believe in one God, the Father almighty, maker of heaven and earth, of all things visible and invisible. I believe in one Lord Jesus Christ, the Only Begotten Son of God, born of the Father before all ages. God from God, Light from Light, true God from true God, begotten, not made, consubstantial with

[25] It is popular among Christians to meet for Bible studies or discipleships in coffee shops. This is where this name comes from.

the Father; through him, all things were made. For us men and for our salvation he came down from heaven, and by the Holy Spirit was incarnate of the Virgin Mary, and became man. For our sake he was crucified under Pontius Pilate, he suffered death and was buried, and rose again on the third day in accordance with the Scriptures. He ascended into heaven and is seated at the right hand of the Father. He will come again in glory to judge the living and the dead and his kingdom will have no end. I believe in the Holy Spirit, the Lord, the giver of life, who proceeds from the Father and the Son, who with the Father and the Son is adored and glorified, who has spoken through the prophets. I believe in one, holy, catholic and apostolic Church. I confess one Baptism for the forgiveness of sins and I look forward to the resurrection of the dead and the life of the world to come. Amen.

I believe in one God, the Father almighty, maker of heaven and earth, of all things visible and invisible. This is naturally the first statement of Christianity. Christians, unlike polytheistic religions, believe in one God who created everything seen and even those things unseen. The authors of this creed first introduce the Father, who is the first member of the Trinity. This is the belief in one God with three parts: the Father, the Son, and the Holy Spirit. The Father, as His name implies, is the prime member. Though all members are equal, they have a hierarchy within themselves. This is one of the most complicated doctrines in Christianity. For a fuller understanding of the Trinity, books dedicated to it would be a better resource than this.

I believe in one Lord Jesus Christ, the Only Begotten Son of God, born of the Father before all ages. The next member of the Trinity, Jesus, is classified as the Son of God. This is not a literal lineage but a title placed upon a few in Scripture, chiefly the angels and those who worship God. Jesus follows the Father like a subject of the Father, but they are equal in power.

God from God, Light from Light, true God from true God, begotten, not made, consubstantial with the Father; through him all things were made. This next part explains the belief in Jesus being one with the Father, no less in power or significance. He was there during creation, and all things were made through Him.

For us men and for our salvation he came down from heaven, and by the Holy Spirit was incarnate of the Virgin Mary, and became man. The next important aspect about Christ is that He is both fully God, as stated above, and fully man. He was born of a virgin, conceived by the Holy Spirit. This is a human impossibility, though not an impossibility for God. Not only was He fully man, but He was also of the lineage of David, making Him a descendant of kings. This was in fulfillment of the promise to David and the prophecies told by the prophets.

For our sake he was crucified under Pontius Pilate, he suffered death and was buried, and rose again on the third day in accordance with the Scriptures. God is the God of justice and love. He loves His creation but requires perfection. He must punish those who left perfection, which is all of us. Since He loves us, He decided to send His Son, the perfect lamb, to die the death of a criminal so that mankind could be with Him again.

He ascended into heaven and is seated at the right hand of the Father. He will come again in glory to judge the living and the dead and his kingdom will have no end. These next two sections go together. After His crucifixion, Christ rose from the dead, conquering death, and is now seated at the right hand of God. The seat to the right of a ruler is the seat of honor. Christ is honored by God because of His sacrifice. The next time

Christ returns will not be as a child unknown to the world but as a conquering king returning to judge the world.

I believe in the Holy Spirit, the Lord, the giver of life, who proceeds from the Father [and the Son], who with the Father and the Son is adored and glorified, who has spoken through the prophets. The Holy Spirit, the third person of the Trinity, is the presence that Christ bestowed on us after His ascension. The Spirit is our new conscious that speaks to us and leads us toward the will of the Father. The Spirit is no less important than the Father or Son, but His role is less obvious. He used to be called the Holy Ghost because it was explained that He possessed a believer with His presence. While the theology is right, the terminology is odd for today's language. The Spirit is who guides us on the path of sanctification.

I believe in one, holy, catholic and apostolic Church. Christians are called to be part of communion with other believers. This is not a suggestion like some believers think. This is a command. Not only are believers to be in communion, but they are also to be a globally unified church. *Catholic* means global.[26] Being a pure, unified Christian force is an important aspect of Christianity. This will be discussed in a later chapter.

I confess one Baptism for the forgiveness of sins, and I look forward to the resurrection of the dead and the life of the world to come. Amen. The ending is one of peace and joy. Because of the sacrifice of Christ and because of the blessing of the Holy Spirit, Christians can now look forward to the resurrection with Christ. They are to be baptized for the declaration of salvation. Baptism in itself does not save, but it is the public statement that believers have accepted the saving grace that Christ has offered.

---

[26] *Definition of Catholic | Dictionary.com.* (n.d.). www.dictionary.com. https://www.dictionary.com/browse/catholic

Salvation by Faith, not Works

The only thing that needs to be added to this creed is salvation by faith. Salvation is not by our works but by our faith. Works-based religions require a person to do altruistic acts, not for the sake of it or out of appreciation but because they are trying to purchase their ticket to heaven.[27] Works-based faiths do not even need the person to want to do the acts. All that matters is that the acts were performed.

While our salvation is by faith through Christ, His works are what save us. Our works cannot save us, but His works can. Christianity is a works-based faith, but unlike other works-based faiths, the works of Christ can only save disciples. His death paid the price. His works satisfied the judgment that was meant for us. No other religion has God sacrifice Himself to save His creation.

Secondary Doctrine

We must believe these primary theologies in our minds, hearts, and mouths to be professing disciples of Christ. If we do not hold to these primary theologies, we are worshiping our own religion. We cannot debate these primary doctrines or replace them. They are the central beam, the core of the faith. Disciples must believe every single one, or they are no longer worshiping the God of the Bible but one of our own making. As stated above, all words of Scripture are important since God took the time to have them put in the Bible. But some doctrines are not pertinent to salvation or for spreading the gospel.

This is where a lot of Neo-Gnostics tend to get hung up. They focus on secondary doctrine as if it was primary doctrine.

---

[27] This does not mean that those in works-based religions do not do their good deeds out of love or kindness. This means that there is an underlying selfish reason. This does not negate the good, only complicates these beliefs.

Since they do not differentiate between these two forms of doctrine, they think that the arguments between denominations is worse than it really is. They think that all parts of Christianity are being argued about when, in reality, we are usually debating about secondary issues.

Coffee Shop Doctrine

We can use baptism as an example of a secondary theology. Baptism is an important concept of Christianity. It is mentioned many times in Scripture[28] and is part of the Great Commission. Christians are to make disciples and baptize them. Making disciples is the first part of the command, and baptizing is the second part. This shows that Christ cares about baptism.

We can see that baptism is an important part of salvation. It is not what saves the person but something that needs to be done to publicly declare salvation. Baptism symbolizes that an individual has died to self and sin and is being resurrected to God. Just like Christ, who died on the cross, was buried in a tomb, and then rose on the third day, baptism shows that an individual is dying to their old evil past and allowing the water to wash away the corruption of this world. It is completely symbolic and has no actual power.

The issue here is that there is a disagreement on how baptism should be done and if it contains any power in itself. Presbyterians believe that sprinkling[29] is theologically accurate, while Baptists believe that immersion[30] is the correct practice. The debate is over verses such as Matthew 3:15–16[31] and He-

---

[28] John 3:23, Acts 2:41, Acts 8:36–38, Colossians 2:12, I Corinthians 10:2, and Matthew 28:19–20

[29] The act of pouring water from a bowl or cup onto the head of a believer

[30] Submerging

[31] But Jesus answered him, "Let it be so now, for thus it is fitting for us to ful-

brews 9:19–22.[32] The verse in Matthew describes Jesus rising out of the water when He was baptized, while Hebrews describes the ancient purification ceremony that utilized blood sprinkling.

The first passage is a key verse used by Baptists, while Presbyterians use the second verse. Both sides have scriptural sources that back up their arguments. This is a debate that has been raging for centuries. The symbolism of death and rebirth is lost in the practice of sprinkling. Yet sprinkling has the symbolism of ancient purification. But in the end, it does not matter which side has more evidence. It only matters that the act is accomplished. Christ calls us to be baptized. He does not lay out explicit instructions on how He desires us to be baptized.

This debate should not fracture churches and definitely should not cause Christians to question salvation.[33] If you want to debate this practice, that is fine. But anything not pertinent to Christ should only be casually discussed.

As discussed in the section on primary theology, theology is important. But it is equally important to understand which doctrines speak on Christ and His nature and which ones dis-

---

fill all righteousness." Then he consented. And when Jesus was baptized, immediately he went up from the water, and behold, the heavens were opened to him, and he saw the Spirit of God descending like a dove and coming to rest on him;

[32] For when every commandment of the law had been declared by Moses to all the people, he took the blood of calves and goats, with water and scarlet wool and hyssop, and sprinkled both the book itself and all the people, saying, "This is the blood of the covenant that God commanded for you." And in the same way he sprinkled with the blood both the tent and all the vessels used in worship. Indeed, under the law almost everything is purified with blood, and without the shedding of blood there is no forgiveness of sins.

[33] The only time that the practice of baptism should be questioned is when it is done for salvation. Those that believe that baptism is required for salvation have walked into the "works" camp. Again, only Christ's works matter, not ours.

cuss everything else. Christianity is about Christ and His works. This is where many Neo-Gnostics get theology wrong. They want it to be about themselves, not Christ. They believe that theology should be about the individual first, and at some point, Christ will be put back in the equation. Christians start with Christ, center on Christ, and end on Christ. He is the first, middle, and last for Christians. Neo-Gnostics, on the other hand, start with themselves, center on the culture around them, and maybe they will add a little bit of Christ's teachings at the end.

Final Remarks

Neo-Gnostics practice a faith of subjective truth, no absolutes, acceptance, and culture over Scripture. If truth is subjective, then anyone can believe what they want. Everyone's truth can be just as true as someone else's truth, even if they contradict. Many of these beliefs stem from post-modernism, which focuses on skepticism, subjectivism, or relativism. This is a Western belief that wants to dismantle, deconstruct, and distrust all ideologies and traditional practices.

"No absolutes" allows anything in life to be questioned. If it is impossible to know something, then we have to allow anything. If life is not concrete, then we can believe anything. Absolutes and objective truths are foreign to the Neo-Gnostic mind.

Since nothing is known and all truths are allowed, Neo-Gnostics believe everything should be accepted. They believe we cannot judge another for their lifestyle, and not only should an individual's lifestyle not be judged, but it should be accepted.

Lastly, culture is the standard by which the past should be judged. The modern culture is more righteous because mankind is in constant social evolution. This evolution allows the goodness within to come out because we are always learning from our ancestors on how to be better. Mankind is naturally good, and it is only the evilness of society that holds love and peace from emerging.

These beliefs have become very popular within the western world in the last fifty or so years. The problem is that they lack any real defenses. Logic, science, history, and theology can be used to combat any belief of the Neo-Gnostic. When it comes to their claims of truth and absolutes, their arguments are simple at best and full of logical errors at worst. Those that argue that truth is subjective are using an objective argument. The same goes with claiming that absolutes are subjective. These statements must use the very things that they are claiming do not exist. But more on that in a different chapter.

When it comes to their beliefs on culture and history, they tend to be grossly misinformed due to their personal ideas of how things should be and what the culture around them teaches. When it comes to morals, there have been cultures worse than ours.[34] But our modern culture has many equal cultures in the moralistic category. Our culture has become very similar to that of Rome. To claim that we have transcended those before us is naive and ignorant.

Theologies of Traditional Christianity

As for traditional Christianity, it is important to know that there are two different types of theologies. One set revolves around Christ and is necessary for salvation. It is necessary because if primary theologies are changed, the god the individual is worshiping will not be the Christian God. It will be a self-created god that has no power.

The other list is full of important items to know and discuss but has nothing to do with salvation. These items are useful for believers to know but believing an incorrect one will not condemn someone to hell. One reason for this is because Scripture

[34] The Assyrians and Aztecs come to mind.

usually backs up two differing views, like immersion or sprinkling for baptism, and this makes it difficult to know exactly which one is true. Also, it has been shown by Scripture that we have an incorrect understanding of something, and Christ will still call us His. This is clear in the story of the thief on the cross (Luke 23:39–43). He was not discipled, he was not baptized, and we have no idea what his beliefs or practices were besides his death as a thief. But he put his faith in Christ, and that is all that mattered.

The important thing is that believers remain humble in their approach to theology. If an individual approaches Scripture humbly, then they are less likely to walk away with a doctrine that was created to suit them. Martin Luther approached Scripture and his issues with the church humbly and patiently. He was not rash and vindictive. He truly desired to find the correct understanding of specific topics, and he was willing to listen and read to discover them. Neo-Gnostics, unlike Luther, desire to find their own paths so that they can travel the road they desire.

Therefore, investigate the faith. Differentiate between primary theologies and secondary theologies. Humbly approach God and listen to His Word. Pick God over culture because culture changes; God never does.

SECTION II

5

Alethiology

Pilate said to him, "What is truth?" After he had said this, he went back outside to the Jews and told them, "I find no guilt in him."

—John 18:38 ESV

Our fourth fork leads us back to a more traversed intersection. When it comes to the study of truth,[1] there are many different views. Many different branches sprout in all sorts of directions. A few of the mouths have boards blocking the path with writing saying things like, "truth is false" or "fools follow truth." It is clear when standing in the middle of the intersection that truth is a very controversial topic. It is controversial because, just like ideology, many other parts of life rest on this one point.

This topic has been heavily debated since man gained enough leisure to ponder such topics. Philosophy in general, and truth in particular, is a very important subject. The way we view truth heavily influences how we see other aspects of life.

[1] Alethiology

In other words, it is central to how we conduct our lives. If we believe that truth is objective, absolute, and has a standard, then our lives will follow a specific path. But, if we believe that truth is subjective, relative, or abnormal, then our lives will look entirely different.

When it comes to truth, there are two primary beliefs individuals can fall under. The first stance is objective truth, and the second is subjective truth. Objective truth is truth that can be proven.[2] Those who follow objective truth believe that all of mankind is held to the same rules no matter the time in history or geographical location. Objective truth was very common during the modernist period. Science and logic ruled the day, and if it could not be explained logically, then it was not true or it was less important. Truth could be found, and once it was, it was necessary to agree with the discovered truth.

Objective truth goes well with scientific studies that require intense investigation and verification. Scientific beliefs such as gravity, gender, and molecular makeup have been proven to such a degree that it is almost impossible to question their validity, at least from a scientific point of view.

Truth pertains not only to science but can also be in philosophy, psychology, religion, or any other subject dealing with mankind and life. From a Christian worldview,[3] objective truth means that if God created the world and established the laws and codes, His ways are truth. This means that no matter what we wish a thing would be or how we wish something would go, certain things will always follow a specific path. Matter will always be matter, carnivores will always choose meat, and

---

[2] "Four Truths." *Human Systems Dynamics Institute,* www.hsdinstitute.org/resources/four-truths.html. Accessed 8 May 2022.

[3] The view of life held by Christians who base their beliefs on Scripture and Christ

Christ will always be the perfect sacrifice for our sins. These truths will never change, nor can they be changed.

Subjective truth, on the other hand, is the opposite of objective truth.[4] This belief focuses on the experiences of the individual.[5] Instead of gravity being a concrete, testable belief, it is the perception of the individual. Or a better example, a person's gender does not come from their anatomical makeup, as science shows, but comes from the inward projection of their subjective experience. Here the perceived subconscious and relative experiences rank higher than what testable science can prove.[6] This belief claims that there are no truths because truth relies more on an individual's experiences than on the external world. Or to put it a different way, all beliefs are true because truth comes from the person's experiences. Here the experience of an individual is the key aspect of truth. Truth for one individual may not be truth for another because their experiences are different. This means that contradicting beliefs can both be true because it is their truth. This leaves subjective truth believers in an interesting spot when someone contradicts them. If they are discussing truth with a person one on one, they tend to be non-confrontational. This is because two truths can coexist no matter the possible contradiction. They can become aggressive if the conversation turns toward systemic issues. If a person disagrees on things like systemic racism or sexism, subjective truth is not so subjective.

---

[4] Obviously

[5] "Four Truths." *Human Systems Dynamics Institute*, www.hsdinstitute.org/resources/four-truths.html. Accessed 8 May 2022.

[6] For honest dialogue, this is not necessarily an incorrect concept. There are areas where a person's experience and belief can rank above science. But these areas lie in non-testable areas. Things like creation or God cannot be tested. Therefore, our perception and experiences can rank higher than what science may say. Here logic reigns, not empirical scientific data.

Objective Truth vs. Subjective Truth

Truth has swung from objective to subjective many times, depending on the period and culture. In today's culture,[7] the debate has veered to the subjective side and is believed to have very little bearing on the average person. This is in direct contrast to the heavy objective stance that the scientific revolution produced. Obviously, our current view on truth is reactionary to the view held by those who lived through the reformation and scientific revolutions. The world of today is unrecognizable compared to the world our great-grandparents lived in.

The belief in subjective truth is not compatible with a Christian's worldview. Christians[8] hold to a strong objective truth stance. As we discussed in the last three chapters, Christianity is a primary ideology and, as such, it has strong beliefs that cannot be removed. This is one reason why Western culture has become strongly anti-Christian.[9] The West claims that there is nothing truly wrong and that all paths can lead to enlightenment and heaven.[10] This is the opposite of what Chris-

---

[7] At least in the post-modern Western world

[8] As any religious view does

[9] During the Roman period, Christians were heavily persecuted socially, economically, physically, and emotionally only because they would not add Caesar to their list of gods. The Romans were very inclusive when it came to religious worship as long as the emperor was also added. Since Christians would not do that (and they acted a little odd in that they would not join in other immoral acts), the rest of the world hated them.

[10] The concept of nothing being wrong does have some limitations, though they tend to change year to year or even month to month. The progressives like to change what is considered wrong or good depending on what organization they are trying to destroy. In the 60s and 70s, it was anything against women and blacks. Then it was anyone against homosexuality. Now it is anyone against the transgender movement. Individuals who were once allies are now deemed evil if they do not continually change their views to match the ever morphing agenda.

tians teach. The primary pillar of Christianity is that Christ is the only way to God.[11] Because of these opposites, Christianity and Western ideology cannot both be correct.

The scientific revolution and the enlightenment produced an overly heavy objective truth stance. It was overly heavy because, as we have mentioned, there are some areas where subjectivity is a thing. One example where subjectivity is a good thing would be opinions. Opinions are feelings that are unverifiable, allowing individuals to express differing thoughts while all being true. Food, sports, music, and movies are all subjective topics. What one individual likes, another dislikes. One claims that a certain movie is the best movie ever made, while another believes the same movie to be garbage. Both of these things are true because they are personal opinions. Opinions are subjective. This is why they are horrible when discussing politics, religion, ethics, or philosophy. When the truly important aspects of life are being discussed, no one wants someone's opinion. They want empirical evidence proving the truth. This is why Thanksgiving dinner can be a nightmare for some. Everyone has an opinion, and in many cases, they are based on nothing but hearsay.

Like most things in life, the pendulum has now swung too far in the opposite direction. During the sixteenth to twentieth centuries, subjectivity was not heavily desired. The newly found freedom to pursue science, theology, and philosophy without strict governmental interference produced a fervor for truth. Now objectivity is not heavily desired. As we discussed in a previous chapter, those who hold to a more post-modernist view see the world as a manmade creation that can be molded to fit whatever ideology a person holds. This can be seen in how the western culture has consistently taken traditional concepts and thrown them away, claiming they are oppressive, pa-

[11] John 14:6

triarchal creations that serve only tyrannical men. This worldview is very subjective and very ignorant.[12]

Truth

This is the study of not only truth but of error as well. This is important because if alethiology investigates truth *and* error, it puts one point in the objective truth category. Logically, there cannot be subjective truth if truth can be objectively rationed. Also, the fact that we have a whole study on this seemingly simple or heavily ignored concept shows that truth is an important subject. Though, it can be allusive at times.

To start, Merriam-Webster defines truth as "the body of real things, events, and facts; a transcendent fundamental or spiritual reality."[13] This means that truth covers both general knowledge as well as philosophical, ethical, and religious realities. Truth can be scientific, historical, mathematical, or even spiritual. This gives it a wide sphere of influence which definitely adds to its complexity.

From the definition above, we can see that truth can be as simple as 2 + 2 = 4, or it can be as complicated as God is the creator of time, yet He is outside of time. This simple to complex range is what makes truth such a difficult thing to study. The average person will agree with a simple truth,[14] but very few will comprehend or even agree with a complicated truth.[15] This

---

[12] There are many examples throughout history that contradict this belief; it just takes some reading.

[13] Merriam-Webster. "Definition of Truth." *Merriam-Webster.com*, 2019, www.merriam-webster.com/dictionary/truth.

[14] Though this is becoming a debated topic by some in the progressive world. What is knowable truth is becoming an unknowable thing to some.

[15] If simple truths are under fire, then it is hard to comprehend how much complicated truths are. Subjective truth is becoming so ingrained in the Neo-Gnostic or progressive worlds that even something like God loving us

is because, as we discussed in the first chapter, most people do not take the time to think about their beliefs on a deeper level. Most people comprehend subjects on a surface level and leave them at that. Objective truth can vary in complexity, and this can make it difficult for people to study.

This leads to the constant battle between subjective and objective truth. If one form of truth can be proven to be objectively true, then other forms of objective truth exist. Therefore, it is our job to work from simple truths all the way to complicated truths. Truth can be studied because truth is objective. No subjective topic can be studied because there is no base to stand on.

If we treat the study of truth like any scientific experiment, we have to find a simple concept and work our way up. As each truth either becomes factual or false, we can slowly sort out this world we live in.[16] We can start with the example of mathematics. Math starts with simple equations like the one above. Math concludes with complex calculus and arithmetic theory. To prove the upper levels of mathematics, we have to prove the lowest forms. This means that we have to prove that two plus two equals four. This may seem like a simple task, but that is the point. We have to prove the simple to prove the complex.

To prove 2 + 2, we can take two sticks and put them in one pile and then take another two sticks and put them in another pile. When we count the sticks, we get four. Thus 2 + 2 has been proved to equal four. Mathematics is just a written language to comprehend nature. We put things like temperature, time, and space in mathematical language. Nature does not know or care much if it is seventy degrees. The passing of time is not written on a stone clock found in nature. We have created the counting

---

can be pushed aside. There are those who hate God so much that their subjective reality says that God cannot love. It does not matter what objective truth one presents their reality says otherwise, and that is all that matters.

16 This is very similar to working through an ideology.

of time to explain an objective reality. Also, a branch does not have markings to show how long it is. We have created length markings to help us know how long something is. Math is a creation to explain nature.

This is how Eratosthenes (276 BC–194 BC) measured the circumference of the earth.[17] By understanding the basics of geometry and the reality of our world, he was able to measure the circumference of the earth. He did this by using the shadow of the sun cast between two cities on the summer solstice. He knew two smaller truths and was able to prove a much bigger truth; the earth is round. This truth had been bouncing around for around three hundred years by the time of Eratosthenes, but he was able to prove mathematically that the hypothesis was true.

Evaluating the Authenticity of a Source

We can take these same types of experiments and use them for the more philosophical quandaries. Though philosophy, ethics, and religion are much harder to prove because we have to look at reality in a much more convoluted field. There are many factors that go into any decision made by a person, and this makes it hard to figure out why they did something. Some of the reasons can be consciously discussed, while many of them may prowl in the subconscious. These subsurface thoughts are sometimes hard to pull up. This makes discovering the truth very difficult.[18]

---

[17] Strom, Caleb. "How Did the Greeks Measure the Earth's Circumference?" *Www.ancient-Origins.net*, www.ancient-origins.net/history-important-events/circumference-earth-0015421. Accessed 22 Sept. 2021.

[18] This should not be confused with the way that Neo-Gnostics tackle things like unconscious racism, sexism, or homophobia. The difference is that the pursuit of truth does not preemptively assume anything. There are things that we subconsciously believe, but they can be very difficult to realize and to assume someone subconsciously believes something is dangerous. This

One thing that can make understanding mankind easier is having a trusted source explain the origin of our complexity. For disciples of Christ, this is Scripture. Scripture explains the beginnings of mankind's evil while giving the root cause. Genesis 1–3[19] explains how mankind was created and how we decided to replace God with ourselves. We took the power of good and evil and made ourselves the source and judge of that power. This explains why our world is so complicated—and so corrupt.

But how do we know that this story is true? We cannot find proof outside of the Bible that this happened. Nor can we recreate it. This means that we have to rely on other factors to prove this story. As we have discussed before, if we can prove that other parts of Scripture are true, we can start to prove the unverifiable parts. The archeological and historical facts that can be proven will also verify stories like creation, the fall of man, and the corruption of our hearts.

We can also use fields like sociology and psychology to show that our hearts and minds are corrupt. We are damaged, hurting, lashing out beings who desire love and peace. The irony is that when we seek love, we do it in a narcissistic way. We tend to focus on ourselves and what we want out of love instead of focusing on our partners and what we can give them. Also, when we seek peace, we tend to create conflict. There are many examples of individuals who so desperately seek love

---

can be seen when looking at racism. If a person believes that all white individuals have an unconscious prejudice, then they are going to see that play out every time they see a bad interaction between individuals of different races. Believing that people have subconscious or unconscious beliefs and assuming all people of a specific type of subconscious or unconscious beliefs are very different things. The first is safe to believe, while the second leads to heavy biases.

[19] Genesis 1–2 are heavily debated as to whether they are literal or poetic descriptions of creation. For our purposes here, this does not matter. What matters is that God created the world, and that we rebelled against Him.

that they drive everyone away with their clinginess and weird behavior.[20] It is easy to understand that we are evil at heart, and it is only through an external savior that we can be freed.

Not the Same Road

Neo-Gnostics, on the other hand, hold certain truths to be absolute while believing in subjective truths. This is a difficult belief to fully understand or defend. They will claim that certain things are evil[21] while saying that all roads lead to God, God does not judge mankind for their sins, and that morals can be subjective. While the actions mentioned are wrong and definitely should not occur, there cannot be absolute wrongs without being absolute truths.

Buddhism, polytheistic paganism, and Christianity cannot all lead to the same road. One leads to nirvana, the other to a myriad of afterlife destinations, and the last to the new heaven and earth or to the lake of burning fire. None of these destinations are even close to each other. This can be compared to a person saying that California, New York, and Florida are all states in America, thus making them basically the same location.

As for God's judgement, this is also incompatible with other religions. Every religion has a list of dos and don'ts that are commanded by the religion's deity. Not one religion is fine with every action possible.[22] The lists may vary, but the concept remains. This shows that judgment is not a subjective religious truth. It can thus be believed that if every religion had a judgment list, Christianity would too. Not only that, one of them has to be right, making the others wrong.

---

[20] This is a very sad phenomenon that is hard to break or change.

[21] Murder, rape, racism, sexism, homophobia, and transphobia

[22] Even Satanism has a list of commandments.

We can see now that this idea of subjective truth is a sham. Truth may be hard to find, but it has to be searched for. If it is not, society starts to crumble, as we see the West doing now. We have to fight for truth no matter how difficult it is to swallow. We have to learn about the Holocaust because it happened, though the Holocaust has come under fire by an ever-growing number of deniers.

We can learn a lot from the pain and suffering the Jews[23] went through. The number of books, movies, and lectures that came from the survivors is astounding. They have lent us their stories to not only tell about the pain but also to show the joy that they have experienced after. The new lives they were given upon freedom gave them such a sense of freedom and excitement for life that they were radically changed. But it is a very horrifying and uncomfortable subject. But truth cannot be ignored. Without truth, nothing is wrong. If nothing is wrong, society will crumble into madness. This may sound dramatic, but we are seeing the effects of subjective truth right now.

Absolutism

The twin to truth is absolutism. This is the idea of an absolute standard or principle.[24] The arguments here are very similar to truth in that there is one side that believes in absolutes and one that believes in ambiguity. Absolutes are those that either are or are not. There is no greyscale in absolutes. The opposite argument does not believe that life has any absolute beliefs. Just like with truth, life is fully ambiguous. Traditional Christians believe in absolutes, while many, if not most, Neo-Gnostics believe in ambiguity.

---

23 And the other groups, though to a much lesser extent

24 "Merriam-Webster Dictionary." *Merriam-Webster.com*, 2022, www.merriam-webster.com/dictionary/absolutism. Accessed 8 May 2022.

An absolute statement is "there are absolutes." The words *is* and *are* are common in these types of arguments. This is because there is no room for a middle ground when something *is*. There *is* a God, life *is* precious, and we *are* children of God. These statements do not allow a grey area. We either are or we are not; there is no maybe.

Another absolute is "there are *no* absolutes." This is what makes the argument against absolutes ironic. To state that there are no absolutes, the speaker has to use an absolute statement. But if the statement "there are no absolutes" is absolute, then there are absolutes. This statement nullifies its own argument. To state in ambiguous terms, the speaker would have to say, "there may or may not be absolutes." But this statement loses all power. We cannot expect anyone to take a *maybe* statement seriously. This is easily seen in how politicians speak. They make many absolute statements about what they are going to do. This makes voters feel confident in their choice. If a politician used more ambiguous statements claiming that they might do something, no one would vote for them. Ambiguous statements are seen as weak, while absolute statements are seen as strong. A soldier talking to an enemy would never say, "I might kill you," because that sounds weak. They would say, "I am going to kill you," because that puts them in a position of authority and strength. This is why opponents of absolutism still speak in absolutes. To do anything else would make them sound weak, and no one would take them seriously. They are operating under the belief that most people will not look deeper into their arguments. However, this is most likely a subconscious thought. Their ploy rests on the laziness of mankind, and it works. We are usually too lazy to investigate philosophy because it is hard. We cannot let hard subjects like philosophy, ethics, math, or any other subject that can be deemed as hard deter us from pursuing them. The tougher the opponent, the sweeter the feeling of victory.

Just like with truth, absolutism is required when discussing right and wrong. To claim that there are actions or beliefs that are never acceptable, there must be an absolute standard. For racism, rape, and homophobia to be wrong, there have to be absolutes. Without an absolute right, there cannot be an absolute wrong. Racism cannot be wrong if there is no such thing as an absolute. If the world operated in relatives, there would be ways to argue for racism. If truth is subjective and there are no absolutes, then Hitler ordering the death of 15–30 million people can be argued as right.[25] This is because we lose all power to judge him because he lived in a different time and a different culture, and he believed that what he was doing was right. Relative truth and ambiguousness say that we cannot judge him for what he did. Objective truth and absolutism can give us the right to say that he was an evil man and that what he did was evil. Truth allows us to condemn the wicked and to fight for the weak. Subjectivity and ambiguousness do not.

For any action to be wrong, it has to be held to a standard. Here standard is referencing some form of law, code, or form of regulation that can be used as a reference. This standard cannot be subjective. If a standard is subjected to culture, time period, or subgroup, then that standard cannot be compared to any other group. This means that racism may be wrong in twenty-first-century America, but it is not wrong in nineteenth to twentieth-century Germany. Living in a world of no absolutes and subjective truth allows for a world where the actions of the Nazis, the Inquisition, and the Atlantic slave trade can all be excused. Subjectivity removes the ability to call something evil. There has to be an absolute, objective truth for there to be evil actions. Sadly, we live in a world where mankind is cruel to each other. We murder, rape, rob, and deceive each other. For

---

25 "Nazi Genocide and Mass Murder." *Hawaii.edu*, 2022, www.hawaii.edu/powerkills/nazis.chap1.htm. Accessed 8 May 2022.

those actions to be called out and stopped, there has to be a base standard to judge everything on.

Moral Relativism

The last argument in the world of relativism/subjectivity pertains to morals. Like the other two beliefs, here there are moral absolutes or relative morals. *Absolute morals* means that there are a set of morals that every individual understands no matter what culture or time in history. A moral absolutist would claim that things like murder, rape, and theft have been wrong in every culture and time in history. This is true. Every culture has some type of cultural expectation to not murder, rape, or steal. What moral absolutists are not saying is that the consequence of these actions is the same. Punishments vary depending on culture and time. But the base moral is the same.

The argument made by Neo-Gnostics is that morals can be subjective. The argument is that mankind in ancient times was more brutal than mankind is today. Some even claim that the Old Testament God was more brutish than the New Testament God. Those that believe this claim that God had some type of personality change or that He changed completely between the Old and New Testaments.

Neo-Gnostics will say that the modern God would not want to cruelly punish His creation. They will also say that some things that were considered wrong were only considered so because of the times. Now that mankind has matured, they can see that those were more barbaric, and it is time to change those restrictions. Some restrictions that need to be changed are on homosexuality, identity, and roles for women. Neo-Gnostics claim that Scripture is too harsh on these groups and that cultural influences are the only reason why they are written in the first place. This means that the passages can be reworked to accommodate modern progress.

The problem is that if mankind has grown more moralistic than their ancestors, then why does mankind still commit every evil today that they did when Christ walked the earth or when God called down the flood? Mankind has remained exactly the same as when Cain killed Abel. The only difference is that mankind has become more sophisticated in its evil than in previous generations. Children are still sacrificed, murder is still common, we commit adultery and fornication, there are still wars, and social hierarchies are still savage to climb.

The twentieth century alone is an example of how cruel mankind can still be. Hundreds of millions of people died due to war, totalitarian regimes, and ideological differences. The war to end all wars (World War I) took about sixty-five million lives by itself.[26] This war was fought because of social Darwinism, nationalism, and the industrial revolution. There were no good reasons to fight this war. To state those three reasons in more simple terms, the war was fought because of racism, pride, and greed.

Another example is abortion. Abortion became legal in the 70s in America and has seen the death of millions of unborn babies.[27] The American child sacrifice is presented on the altar of individuality, personal freedom, promiscuity, lust, and pride.[28]

We claim that our culture has transcended the evils of our ancestors. In reality, we have just sophisticated our evils. Instead of worshipping gods like Ares, Aphrodite, and Gaea, we

---

26 "Casualties of World War I." Facing History and Ourselves, 2018, www.facinghistory.org/weimar-republic-fragility-democracy/politics/casualties-world-war-i-country-politics-world-war-i.

27 Dorman, Sam. "An Estimated 62 Million Abortions Have Occurred since Roe v. Wade Decision in 1973." *Fox News*, 22 Jan. 2021, www.foxnews.com/politics/abortions-since-roe-v-wade.

28 There are those who abort a child out of fear, coercion, or ignorance. But to many abort for the reasons mentioned above.

worship social justice, casual sex, and environmental extremism.

Nothing New

> *What has been is what will be, and what has been done is what will be done, and there is nothing new under the sun.*
>
> —Ecclesiastes 1:9 ESV

It has been stated before, but it will be stated again: there is nothing new in this world. King Solomon, who is considered the wisest man on earth, is the one who wrote the verse above. Three thousand years ago, he wrote that there would be nothing new. This means that all beliefs and all practices have been believed or practiced. Many individuals today believe that the post-modern view on deconstruction and relativism are new concepts. But the ancients were just as relative, subjective, and anti-establishment as some are today.

John 18:38[29] shows clearly that post-modern questioning had already made its way to first-century Roman politicians. We like to claim that our views are modern and progressive when, in reality, we are constantly cycling through the same thoughts over and over again. Greek philosophers argued about relative truth, Pilate believed in relative truth, and once again, Neo-Gnostics believe in relative truth.

The true irony about Pilate's statement is that he declares to the crowd that he finds no guilt in Him. To find guilt, there must be a standard to measure Him by. While Pilate thought that he did not believe in truth, he still judged under an abso-

---

[29] Pilate said to him, "What is truth?" After he had said this, he went back outside to the Jews and told them, "I find no guilt in him."

lute truth. We may say out loud that we do not believe in truth, but our lives show everything but.

Scripture Is Truth

Disciples of Christ follow Scripture not because it has truth but because it is Truth. This can be seen in John 17:17.[30] In Greek, there are multiple words for *truth*. One form is *alethenos*[31] or *alethes*, which is the adjective for truth.[32] If Christ used these forms, He would have been saying that scripture was true, something to be put beside other truthful things. But this is not the form that Jesus uses here. Here Jesus uses the word *aletheia*,[33] which is the noun form.[34] Christ is saying that Scripture is the truth. The truth above all other truths.

If Scripture is the truth, then believers need to put it above all other things. As we have discussed so far, if truth is objective, there are absolutes, and morals are absolute, there has to be a standard that these things are measured by. God is the standard and the judge, and we find His standards written in Scripture.

If Scripture holds the absolute standards, and Scripture was inspired by God, then Scripture can be proven to be truth. This is why Jesus compares Scripture to Himself. If God is truth,[35] and Scripture has been declared truth by Jesus,[36] and

---

30 Sanctify them in the truth; your word is truth.

31 "Strong's Greek: 228. ἀληθινός (Aléthinos) -- True." *Biblehub.com*, 2022, biblehub.com/greek/228.htm. Accessed 8 May 2022.

32 "Strong's Greek: 227. ἀληθής (Aléthés) -- True." *Biblehub.com*, 2022, biblehub.com/greek/227.htm. Accessed 8 May 2022.

33 This is the where we get the term *alethiology*.

34 "Strong's Greek: 225. ἀλήθεια (Alétheia) -- Truth." *Biblehub.com*, 2022, biblehub.com/greek/225.htm. Accessed 8 May 2022.

35 John 14:6

Jesus is God,[37] then Jesus is putting Scripture almost at the same level as Himself. The words of an individual are always held to the same position as the individual. A king's words were equal to law in certain cultures. This is because their words were equal to themselves, and they were the law. God is the same. He and His declarations are equal only because He stated them. Scripture is His words; this is why it is held so highly. To be clear, we do not worship Scripture. While it is the Word of God, it is not God. It is a finger pointing to God.

This is why scriptural inerrancy is so important. Any mistake in Scripture cascades up to God Himself. If Scripture is not truth, then God is not truth. If God is not truth, then He is not worth worshipping. The entire concept crumbles with the crumbling of Scripture.

Ending Remarks

When it comes to life, truth is one of the most important foundations. Everything we do or believe stems from what we believe to be true. When the earth was believed to be flat, we did not sail in specific directions; when we did not know about germs, doctors had no problem not washing their hands between patients; and when we did not understand science, we thought flies were spontaneously created in feces. Finding truth can radically change the way a person thinks or acts.

If we live by subjective truth, we are fine with others living lives that can be harmful to them. Promiscuous sex becomes a normal thing because their truth says that it is fine. Objective truth says that fornication can lead to STIs, AIDs, depression, and family instability. Life has consequences, and understanding the objective reality can alleviate those consequences. But

---

[36] John 17:17

[37] Mark 14:61–62

since we live in a society that does not want to hurt a person's feelings, we rather allow them to live in their own subjective truth even if it is damaging them. Neo-Gnostics want to live in this subjective world, but reality does not really care about subjectivity. It does not care if someone believes that sleeping around is fine, and it will not change its consequences to accommodate the individual's subjective experiences.

On top of not wanting to deal with objective truth, Neo-Gnostics like to live in a world where nothing is absolute. This includes both truth and morals. This does sound nice at first, but like most horror movies, the charming town is full of ghouls at night. We have to have absolutes, or nothing in nature or life works. Gravity is an absolute. Gravity will pull anything back to earth. That is a fact. There are things that are wrong, and there are things that are right. Murder is wrong, adultery is wrong, and slavery is wrong. These are all wrong things. But for them to be wrong, there has to be an absolute standard that they can be judged by. This standard has to be resolute and cannot change based on culture or experience. An experience may explain an action, but it does not justify it. A husband cheating on his wife may explain why she stabbed him, but it does not justify it. A workaholic husband may explain why his wife cheated on him, but it does not justify her actions. An army conquering another people may explain why they enslaved them, but it does not justify the action. This standard treats all people in all situations the same. Absolutes create a right and a wrong. Without them, evil cannot be called evil, and good cannot be called good.

Right and wrong are deep issues, and they cannot be dealt with lightly. A person may steal to feed his family, but does that make stealing right? The food he steals might put the shop owner in a position where he cannot feed his family. Or he might lose his shop because he cannot pay for the ingredients.[38]

[38] This is not trying to simplify complicated situations. There are times when

Or for a more cinematic example, Thanos (the villain from Marvel Comics) desired to heal the world. He believed that there were too many people in the universe[39] and that something needed to be done. He believed that the resources in the universe were being overtaxed and that population reduction was the right choice to solve this problem. He thought that by reducing the universe's population by half, the rest could live better lives. Deep down, the problem that he saw was a true one, and he was truly trying to help people. But his solution was still evil. Slaughtering millions or billions or trillions of people so that others may live is not a good solution. He was still murdering countless souls to achieve his philanthropic goal.

The only way to know that the actions taken in both examples are wrong is because there is an absolute standard. This standard shows what is right and what is wrong. Even though Thanos had a solution to solve the universe's problem, the Avengers realized that murder, even for a righteous reason, is still murder. Murder is absolutely wrong, no matter the reason. Logic also helps in most situations. But to be honest, life is complicated, and sometimes it is hard to know what is right or wrong. Luckily this is why believers are given the Holy Spirit. God will guide us through difficult situations. God helps navigate us through the complexities of right and wrong.

---

one wrong thing is excused because of the specific situation. Rahab lied to save the lives of the Jewish spies in Jericho. But she lied for God; her action was forgiven, and she was even blessed by being an ancestor to Christ. There are times when God excuses an action because we were trying to put Him first. This is why there is an argument about whether those who were trying to save the Jews during the Holocaust should have lied. Lying is wrong no matter what, but some would argue that there are times when it can actually be excused.

[39] This is very similar to Malthus's belief in our overpopulation that has led to many horrible policies.

Stand for What We Believe In

We can no longer let the fear of hurting someone's feelings stop us from telling them the truth. Real love is doing the hard thing so that life can be better. If we truly thought that those who do not have a relationship with God are going to hell, we would share the gospel with everyone. If we truly thought that living an immoral life was damaging, we would be less reserved when discussing morals with people. The truth is that even if we believe the things discussed in this book, we are too scared of losing a friend or of looking like a crazy person to stand for what we believe. We rather let people live destructive lives than hurt their feelings or lose a friend.

Life is hard enough when we are not called to live a more restrictive version by God. We add on even more restrictions because we are trying to live for Christ. This makes Christianity a heavy burden that can only be carried with the strength of Christ. Those who think that following Christ is supposed to lead to an easy life were told the wrong gospel. God is truth, and to stand in its light can make others hate us. But it is worth it to be in that light.

Life is full of truths. But there is only one truth. This truth is God and comes from His Word. Since His Word has been inspired by Himself, it is considered truth. This means that we need to obey it as if it was given to us directly from God (because it has been).

Truth is important, as stated many times in this chapter, but if we do not obey the truth, then our lives will be left to wander in pursuit of the truth. God has given us a direct guide to Him. He even came down as Christ to point the way. We have the Spirit continually guiding us. All of these things are to help us stay on the narrow path. God's truth is narrow, but with His help and strength, it is possible to stay on that path.

6

Love

You shall love the Lord your God with all your heart and with all your soul and with all your mind. This is the great and first commandment. And a second is like it: You shall love your neighbor as yourself.

—Matthew 22:37–39 ESV

Our last intersection may not be commonly thought about, but this intersection is very popular. There are paths going in every conceivable direction, but only one can keep us on the narrow path we desire to travel, even more so than intersections before. The concept of love, which is what the sign above reads, like truth, is something that we tend to take for granted. Everyone has a belief in love, and they tend to vary wildly. Some believe in an all-accepting type of love. Here there is no judgment, just love. Others, on the other hand, believe in a more tough love, believing that love should be more ridged. Here love is strict and does not allow for any change. There are even those that do not believe that love exists or if it does, it should be rarely shown. Some give love out like Santa Clause around Christmas, while others hold onto it like Ebenezer Scrooge with his money.

Since there are so many different views on love, how are we to differentiate between authentic love and fake love? Is it even possible to find a baseline to start from, as we have done in our other chapters? The answer to both questions is a solid yes. There is a way to tell between real love and fake love, and we can find a baseline for love. This will, like everything else, be shown by looking at Scripture. God is very clear on how we are to love and who we are to love.[1] Traditional Christians practice a sacrificial love, while Neo-Gnostics practice a self-love. Sacrificial love focuses on others and what they need, while self-love focuses on the individual and what they desire over others.

Now the first step in differentiating between Neo-Gnostic and traditional Christian love, and the two types of love mentioned above, is to break down the word itself. This means that we need to discuss the different varieties of love. While this can be a difficult task when it comes to the English language, it is not impossible. We only have one real word to describe strong affection, and that is *love*. But that does not mean that we do not have other words that we use to describe similar actions or affections. We use words like compassionate, erotic, and brotherly to describe other forms of love. While they may be uncommon, they are still used. One better way of looking at love is recognizing how other languages use it.

Other languages, like Greek, have multiple words denoting different types of love. Unlike English, theirs are very common and used for specific forms of love. Each word has a specific meaning and allows the speaker to differentiate what they are feeling. Sadly, since English has been a global language for so long, it has become simplified. American English has definitely

---

[1] It is very true that Christians throughout history have misused God's words to further their own agendas. There have been individuals in the church who believed that interracial marriage was unbiblical. This is a drastic warping of God's word and has no place in the church.

been simplified over the centuries due to the number of individuals adapting and changing the language.[2]

Instead of using only one word for love, Greek has *philia, eros,* and *agape*. These are only three words in the Greek language for love, but that will suffice for this chapter. There are two reasons why we are going to use the Greek forms of love instead of another language. First, the Western world has been heavily influenced by Greek culture.[3] Second, the New Testament was written in Greek. When Paul, Luke, and the other authors wrote the New Testament, they did it in Greek. This means that if we understand the original words used in the New Testament, it will make our job of understanding God's form of love that much easier. Unfortunately, there are some things that can get muddied in translation. This is why it is important to stick as close to the original as possible.

Let Them Speak Greek

While there is a lot to say about the influential power of Greek culture on history, it cannot be correctly summed up here. That is an entire historical subject that could take volumes to fully explore. With that said, we can skip over the first reason to look at Greek and jump directly into the second reason. We will start our linguistic discussion with philia.

---

[2] Many parts of American English have been boiled down to the easiest usage possible. As immigrants migrated to America, it became easier to use simpler forms of words instead of the more poetic forms used in England. In the Hellenistic period (when Greek was the global language of trade), the Greeks did not let their language become as muddied as English users have.

[3] Greek culture influenced the Romans, who in turn influenced the Germanic tribes and the Celts. The Anglo-Saxons, Normans, and Vikings have all had a role in creating modern day England, and they were almost all influenced by the Greeks in one way or another.

Philia comes from the root philos and means friendship, affection, fondness, and love.[4] This type of love is usually called brotherly love. The city Philadelphia is named after this meaning because it was meant to be the city of brotherly love.[5] This form of love is used in James 4:4.[6] Philia is not a commonly used word in Scripture. Strong's dictionary only has it listed once.

Eros is kind of the opposite of philia. It means more of a physical, sexual love.[7] Eros was actually a Greek god of love which does show how much the ancient Greeks liked this form of love. He was either a primordial being[8] or the son of Aphrodite, depending on the version.[9] We get words like erotic from this word, which due to its sexual nature, is why there is a slightly negative connotation to it. Interestingly, Strong's dictionary has no reference to this form of love in Scripture.

The last form of love is *agape* or *agapeo*. This is the most commonly referenced form of love from Scripture. This form of love means to take pleasure in, long for, with benevolence and esteem.[10] This form of love can be found in verses like Matthew

---

4 "Strong's Greek: 5373. φιλία (Philia) -- Friendship." *Biblehub.com*, biblehub.com/greek/5373.htm. Accessed 25 Sept. 2021.

5 This meant that everyone, no matter their religion, class, or skin color, could live there and be treated as an equal.

6 You adulterous people! Do you not know that friendship with the world is enmity with God? Therefore whoever wishes to be a friend of the world makes himself an enemy of God.

7 Definition of Eros | Dictionary.com." *www.dictionary.com*, 2019, www.dictionary.com/browse/eros.

8 Being the son of Chronos, who was one of the most powerful beings in the universe

9 The Editors of Encyclopedia Britannica. "Eros | Greek God." *Encyclopædia Britannica*, 9 Aug. 2018, www.britannica.com/topic/Eros-Greek-god.

10 "Strong's Greek: 26. ἀγάπη (Agapé) -- Love, Goodwill." *Biblehub.com*, biblehub.com/greek/26.htm. Accessed 25 Sept. 2021.

24:12[11], Romans 13:10[12], and John 3:16[13]. Agapeo has been explained as undeserved love. This is where the benevolent definition would come into play. The idea is that we did not deserve love, but God gave it anyway.

Agapeo is the most commonly used form of love in the New Testament. It, or a form of it, is used more than 259 times (Matthew 5:43, Matthew 19:19, and Luke 6:27, to name a few).[14] Out of all the forms of love, God chose to use this specific form abundantly. One occurrence is just a small thought. A few occurrences are just small hints. Over two hundred occurrences are an undeniable statement. God wanted it to be very clear which form of love He was talking about.[15]

But just because this form of love is used abundantly, how are we to know exactly what God meant by undeserving love? That is a great question, and luckily Scripture gave us two examples to demonstrate this type of love. First, God sent His son to die for us, and second, Jesus gives us the story of the Good Samaritan.

---

11 And because lawlessness will be increased, the love of many will grow cold.

12 Love does no wrong to a neighbor; therefore love is the fulfilling of the law.

13 For God so loved the world, that he gave his only Son, that whoever believes in him should not perish but have eternal life.

14 "How Many Words Are There in the Greek Language for Love?" *NeverThirsty*, 16 June 2015, www.neverthirsty.org/bible-qa/qa-archives/question/how-many-words-are-there-in-the-greek-language-for-love/#:~:text=AGAPE%20is%20the%20most%20common%20word%20for%20love. Accessed 25 Sept. 2021.

15 This is where translational issues really come into play. We can understand that God is talking about love no matter the translation. The issue is that we cannot know the type of love. Just like we discussed back in chapter two, to understand context, we sometimes have to know the form of the word. We cannot truly understand God if we do not know what He has said. We cannot know what He has said if we do not do our research and pursue Him.

Love Like Jesus First Loved Us

God never expects us to do anything without Him doing it first. He expects us to be perfect because He is perfect; He expects us to love unconditionally because He has loved unconditionally. This is clearly seen through the life of Jesus. He came into this world not in riches and comfort but in meekness and in poverty. He was born into the family of a carpenter. Joseph (Jesus's earthly father) would not have been dirt-poor, being that he was a skilled craftsman, but he would not have been rich by any means. In modern terms, he would most likely have been lower middle class. He was your solid blue-collared working man.

Jesus grew up like any other Jewish boy in the first century A.D. We assume that He went to Synagogue and did most other things that kids His age would have done. But when He started His mission is when things got interesting. The last three years of His life are where Christianity puts all of its attention.

There are three main areas where Jesus showed unconditional love. First, He healed the sick of their physical and spiritual ailments. Those who society had put aside, he focused on. He did this by physically healing leprosy[16] and the disabled and by forgiving sins.[17]

---

[16] Leprosy is a physical ailment that damages the pain nerves. While that does not sound too bad at first, it can have life ending consequences. This disease does not allow the person to feel pain; therefore people hurt themselves without even knowing it. They burn themselves, cut off fingers, or do any sort of physical harm. This causes people to basically fall apart.

[17] "While he was in one of the cities, there came a man full of leprosy. And when he saw Jesus, he fell on his face and begged him, 'Lord, if you will, you can make me clean.' And Jesus stretched out his hand and touched him, saying, 'I will; be clean.' And immediately the leprosy left him. And he charged him to tell no one, but 'go and show yourself to the priest, and make an offering for your cleansing, as Moses commanded, for a proof to them.'" —Luke 5:12–14 (ESV)

Second, He associated with the outcast and dejected. Not only did He heal those who were cast out of society, but He also ate and talked with those that society had deemed undeserving. This included tax collectors, prostitutes, and other sinners.[18] Jesus believed that it was His duty to show love to all, not just the righteous. He actually believed that those who were unrighteous deserved His attention more than the righteous.[19] Jesus was quite clear: He came for the sinners of the world. The writing between the words is that all of us are sinners. The only difference between the religious and the sinners is that one group still understood they needed a savior, and the other group had crafted their own savior. We all need a savior, but some have crafted a religion and savior that fit their own agenda.

The third and last example is His death. Christ loved the undeserving so much that He put down His own life so that we could live again. Luckily it was not a permanent death since He is God, but the action does not lose any of its power. He died for our sins and rose again, slaying the master that had a hold on us—death.

God is a perfect being, and because of this, He cannot withstand imperfection. When we ate of the fruit and cast ourselves into damnation, He made a way to bring us back to Himself. That gap could not be breached by our own power. The law shows this very clearly. The only way to bring us back was to offer a perfect sacrifice. The only way was for Christ to live that perfect life and die in our place.

His love of the disabled is beautiful. His love of the outcast is beautiful. But nothing compares to the unconditional, sacrificial love that He showed on the cross. He endured the ultimate

---

[18] "And the Pharisees and their scribes grumbled at his disciples, saying, 'Why do you eat and drink with tax collectors and sinners?'" —Luke 5:30 (ESV)

[19] "And Jesus answered them, 'Those who are well have no need of a physician, but those who are sick. I have not come to call the righteous but sinners to repentance.'" —Luke 5:31–32 (ESV)

pain and humiliation, both before man and God, so that He could have us near God and Himself. That is love. There is nothing we can do to repay Him, and He desires nothing in return but our complete and unflinching love.

The next example is not as powerful, but it is an example given to us by Christ in the gospels. If Christ's sacrifice is not enough of an example, we can look at the example that He gave us on how to love.

Love Like the Good Samaritan

The story of the Good Samaritan[20] has been mentioned before in this book. But it is now time to dive a little deeper than we have before. When Christ told this story, He told it in a very strategic way. First, He blatantly contrasts the Samaritan with the religious elite. Next, He gives very few details about the mugged Jew. Lastly, He does not give any details about the Samaritan. All we are told is that an enemy of the Jewish man was the only person willing to help him. But what is left out speaks volumes.

God is showing that He does not care about race, class, sexuality, identity, political beliefs, or religious beliefs when it comes to showing love. God is stating clearly that when it comes to loving others, we are to just love. Love with an agapeo type of love. Love that sacrifices for another. Agapeo does not judge, does not require anything in return, and does not care

[20] "But he, desiring to justify himself, said to Jesus, 'And who is my neighbor?' Jesus replied, 'A man was going down from Jerusalem to Jericho, and he fell among robbers, who stripped him and beat him and departed, leaving him half dead... But a Samaritan, as he journeyed, came to where he was, and when he saw him, he had compassion. He went to him and bound up his wounds, pouring on oil and wine. Then he set him on his own animal and brought him to an inn and took care of him. And the next day he took out two denarii and gave them to the innkeeper, saying, 'Take care of him, and whatever more you spend, I will repay you when I come back.'" — Luke 10:29–37 (ESV)

about man-made differences.[21] We set up class differences, race differences, and cultural differences.[22] To God, we are all His children, and He desires for us to love each other as He has loved us.

God's love is shown in three specific ways in this story. First, he transcended prejudice. We discussed this point above. Second, he loved with his time. Time has always been a precious thing. We like to think that our time is more precious now than it was hundreds or thousands of years ago. But in reality, their time was most likely more precious. It took more work to do anything in ancient times. Water did not come from a spigot in the kitchen, food was not wrapped nicely in a giant store ready to be stored for days at a time, and they did not have powerful machines that could transport them anywhere in a short amount of time. Journeys were slow, cumbersome, and dangerous. As the story states, the traveler had been mugged on his travels. This means that when the Samaritan stopped and helped him, he was putting his own life at risk.[23]

Trips also could take weeks or months to complete, and taking the time to bandage the Jewish man, transport him to an inn, and pay to keep him there would have taken a lot of time that the Samaritan would have probably rather used on his trip.

This leads us to the last thing; he gave up his money. We are never told the economic status of the Samaritan. Was he poor or rich? We will never know. Either way, he was willing to

---

[21] As we discussed in chapter one, the Samaritan and the Jew had cultural and religious differences. They had been culturally enemies for a long time by this point.

[22] This is a big problem with Neo-Gnostics. Progressives are falling fully for the idea that different races should be treated differently. A white person should be treated one way while a black person another. This is a dangerous belief and will always lead to social conflict and deteriation.

[23] It is a practice used by highway thieves to use a helpless person to draw in others who are coming to assist. The Samaritan would have known this, and he took the chance anyway.

give up precious resources to help a cultural enemy that he had never met. He gave up medical supplies as well as his finances. Bandages could have come from his personal medical stash, or it could have been his actual clothing, we are not told. But he was willing to give up his personal belongings to assist this fallen individual.

This is the type of love that God is calling His people to. He wants His followers to be willing to give up anything and everything for Him and for their neighbors. We are supposed to be willing to walk the extra mile or give up our coats to love both our neighbor and our enemy.

This is directly opposite of what Neo-Gnosticism teaches. As we discussed in chapter one, Neo-Gnostics practice something called *self-love*. As we discussed then, *self-love* puts the needs of the individual over the needs of others. This is never done blatantly, nor is it ever stated in this way. But their actions betray their inner meaning. A common phrase used for *self-love* is "I just need to take care of me right now." While caring for one's needs can be very important, the Samaritan did not put himself first. We should care for ourselves, but it should not be our initial go-to every time a person needs help. Neo-Gnostics and our modern culture, in general, put little time into helping others.

It usually starts slow. First, they will remove individuals around them who they claim are only using them, and then they will slowly start cutting out other forms of charitable actions. Eventually, they are left helping no one but themselves.[24]

---

[24] While we do need to be good stewards of our time and money, there is a big difference between the way Christ calls us to steward and how Neo-Gnostics practice it. The easiest way to state it is that the bar is drastically higher for Christians then it is for Neo-Gnostics.

Love God to Love Our Neighbors

This whole concept of how true love is supposed to be is summed up in one concise statement by Jesus. In a conversation with a Jewish lawyer[25,26] Christ shows that true love only has two parts. First, we are to love God. Love Him with everything that we have, our mind, our body, and our soul. Secondly, we are to love our neighbor.

An important part of this is that we cannot truly love our neighbor until we love God. This is because if we try to love those around us before God or without God, it will always turn into a selfish love. We love ourselves first no matter what we do. But, only through the grace and power of God can we ever truly love those around us.

Secondly, we are to love our neighbor as the Good Samaritan loved. Christ used this story to show the lawyer what God expects when it comes to loving others. Once we love God, we can then love those around us. One big group we are called to love is sinners. One reason we need to love sinners is that we are sinners.

No to Sin, Yes to The Sinner

Another key element of love is differentiating between sin and sinner. It has always been and will always be a difficult conundrum. On the one hand, we tend to identify ourselves by our sin. Because of this, we tend not to like it when someone says

---

25 The conversation that prompted the story of the Good Samaritan

26 "Teacher, which is the great commandment in the Law?" And he said to him, "You shall love the Lord your God with all your heart and with all your soul and with all your mind. This is the great and first commandment. And a second is like it: You shall love your neighbor as yourself. On these two commandments depend all the Law and the Prophets." —Matthew 22:36–40 (ESV)

that they love us but not our sin. Sin leeches onto our very being, and instead of being a part of us, it becomes all of us. This is why loving sinners but hating sin is almost an impossible task.

When it comes to Neo-Gnostics, they tend to go too far and accept the sin so they can love the sinner. Obviously, we cannot reduce the sin to make ourselves feel better. God is wholly against sin. We have not been given the authority to change God's law or standard. What they are trying to do is a good thing. Their desire is to bring people to God. The issue is that we can never bring people to Him. He is the only one who can do that. We are supposed to bring the gospel to them; that is all.[27] Their heart is in the right place. But their understanding of God, His character, and His plan are wrong.

Neo-Gnostics focus more on the power of man and our ability to change the heart of a person and forget that we cannot change the person. They desire to bring sinners to God by allowing the person to reach God as they are. God is love, justice, and grace, meaning that we cannot approach God as we are. We have to change and orient ourselves toward Christ. They forget that this is not about us but about Christ. This makes evangelism almost impossible because we need to understand who we are in comparison to God, not to ourselves.

On the other hand, traditional Christians hate the sinner so that they can hate the sin. We are called to love the sinner but hate the sin as we have mentioned before. The issue here is that we are throwing the baby out with the bathwater, so to speak. Instead of showing mercy and love, as Christ did, and then removing the thorn, we have reversed it. Christians try to remove the thorn of sin,[28] and then they show God's love and mercy.

---

[27] Why exactly we are to do this is unclear. The best argument is 1) because God wants to include us in His plan of redemption, and 2) He told us to do it. It is as simple as that.

[28] Which will never be fully accomplished in this life

They do this by forcing people to live holy lives with the belief that living righteously can get a person into heaven. This becomes legalism and is deemed just as evil to Christ as the other side.[29]

It is clear by Christ's ministry that we are not to expect change and then show love. Christ showed love, and then He told us to follow Him. The fact that the entire story of redemption is based on the idea that we cannot come to Christ without Him coming to us first shows that He loved and then told us to repent. We are to love and then expect external change. Not the other way around. A great example of this is in Matthew 18:23–33.[30] We see that a king is settling his debts with those in his realm. One servant owes him quite a lot of money and cannot pay it back. The servant is spared out of the king's mercy but does not show that same mercy to another servant that owes him money.

The story can be summed up like this: God has redeemed an unimaginable debt from us; therefore, we need to show that same kind of mercy and love to others.

---

[29] Matthew 23:13–39

[30] "Therefore the kingdom of heaven may be compared to a king who wished to settle accounts with his servants. When he began to settle, one was brought to him who owed him ten thousand talents. And since he could not pay, his master ordered him to be sold, with his wife and children and all that he had, and payment to be made. So the servant fell on his knees, imploring him, 'Have patience with me, and I will pay you everything.' And out of pity for him, the master of that servant released him and forgave him the debt. But when that same servant went out, he found one of his fellow servants who owed him a hundred denarii, and seizing him, he began to choke him, saying, 'Pay what you owe.' So his fellow servant fell down and pleaded with him, 'Have patience with me, and I will pay you.' He refused and went and put him in prison until he should pay the debt… Then his master summoned him and said to him, 'You wicked servant! I forgave you all that debt because you pleaded with me. And should not you have had mercy on your fellow servant, as I had mercy on you?' — Matthew 18:23–33 (ESV)

Why We Must Love

There are two other problems that arise from this issue. Primarily many individuals do not want to be loved unless their sin is accepted. It is not our job to force a person to accept our love. It is our job to love. If we show love and they do not accept, that is on them, not us. We followed God's command.

Christ spent most of His ministry conversing and eating with sinners. He came to help the sick, not the healthy. Now we are not Christ, but we are to be Christ-like. He did do things that we cannot do, but we can love the way He loved. We may have to be more careful in what situations we get into, but that cannot be a reason why we do not love. Scripture tells us to be discerning and to live above reproach.[31] Love cannot be a casualty of living an above reproach life.

Scripture is clear about how we are to view sin. We know how to view sin because it tells us how God views it. We are to hate sin like God hates sin. God despises sin because it is the opposite of who He is. Just like darkness cannot be in the presence of light, sin cannot be in God's presence. This is because sin is the complete opposite of what God is and who He is. The power of His perfection obliterates the corruption of sin and anything that possesses it.

But God sent His son to die on the cross for us. He died so that we could be reunited with Him again. Jesus loved us so much, with agapeo love, that He was willing to come to earth, live a perfect life, die in one of the most painful executions mankind has ever conceived, be separated from the Father, rise

---

[31] If an individual is trying to start a ministry assisting prostitutes, there is a mature way in doing it. A man going into brothels is not the way to do it. There are smart ways to tackle sensitive issues. Christ had many followers and conversed and ate with many people outside of their place of work. Setting up a public place for prostitutes and the like to go is a much safer and smarter path.

again after three days, and then ascend to heaven again just for us.

That is one of the most selfless acts mankind could ever dream of. That is love. He was willing to do all of that while we were considered His enemies (Romans 5:10).[32] If God was willing to do all of this for people who despised Him, why cannot we love people who, at best, like us and, at worst, want to kill us? Jesus died for people who did kill Him. The least we can do is love those who are neutral to us.

God may hate the sin of sinners, and He may have to judge them one day, but He still loves them. In *The Cost of Discipleship*, Dietrich Bonhoeffer put it this way: "May we be enabled to say 'no' to sin and 'yes' to the sinner."[33] All sinners are worth loving since Christ felt that they were worth dying for. Christ did not tell us any attributes of who not to love. He did not say not to love a drunkard, a gambler, a prostitute, a philanderer, a homosexual, or any other thing He considers sinful. We are to love them.

Love the Person, Not the Lifestyle

This does not mean that their sinful actions are to be glossed over. There is a difference between loving a person and accepting their lifestyle. Christ made it very clear that He did not approve of the lifestyle that sinners led. But He made it also clear that all sins are equal in His eyes.[34] The corrupt religious leader's lifestyle was just as abhorrent to Him as the greedy tax collector or the prostitute. But even though they knew that He did

[32] For if while we were enemies we were reconciled to God by the death of his Son, much more, now that we are reconciled, shall we be saved by his life. —Romans 5:10 (ESV)

[33] Bonhoeffer, Dietrich. *The Cost of Discipleship*. New York, Touchstone, 2012, p. 39.

[34] James 2:10, Romans 2:11

not approve of their lifestyle, Jesus made it very clear as well that He was willing to associate with them, love them, and die for them. To take this a step further, Christ actually spent more time with "vile" sinners than He did with the religious. Christ hated those who thought they were saved by the law.

Now the way we show that we dislike the lifestyle or actions while loving the individual is the difficult part. There is no one approach to deal with this issue, but that does not mean we cannot try. One good method is making churches and church groups more comfortable for individuals who have not embraced Christ. There is a big difference between being a part of a church/Christian community and someone who just goes to a church/Christian community.

Those who are part of a church need to be fully invested in Christ and orient their lives toward Him. He is not our number one; He is our only one. There are many individuals who do not participate in Christ's mission but are a part of a church. They are the lukewarm believers that Christ will spit out. It is common for these types of "believers" to form churches where everyone who attends is of the same temperature. This is why it can be hard to find a good church. Some places[35] are so overpopulated by church buildings that one could spend a year visiting them all and never attend a church twice. The issue is that most of these churches are lukewarm. This means that we need to differentiate between believers and attendees.

With this distinction, we can make room for those who are saved and serving Christ and those who are observing and interested in Christ. Christ did not force His message onto anyone. He actually made it harder for people to come to Him. This can be seen when Christ discusses how the thought of hate or lust was equal to the actual sin.[36] The message is open to every-

---

[35] Like the South in America

[36] Matthew 5:21–30

one,[37] and we need to create spaces to allow anyone to show up. Too many times, we are the stumbling block, not Christ.

Love is not the end all be all, but it is very important. We need to remove as many barriers as possible so that the gospel can reach as many as possible. There are many barriers that cannot be lowered, but there are also too many ridiculous barriers that the church has erected to make itself feel better. These types of barriers are the same as the ones that Christ rebukes the Pharisees for. We like to force people onto a road of our making before they can even get on God's path. We do this by creating additional laws to make a person pure in our eyes. We take command of God's Word and add to it until it fits our own ideology.

This is where primary theology plays its part. Too many secondary doctrines are forced upon people as primary doctrine before they can be considered believers. This is not loving, nor is it theologically correct. We cannot force our opinions on people when they are opinions, not dogma.

Unconditional Love or Unconditional Acceptance

Up until this point, we have discussed different types of love, how Christ showed us how to love, and how we are to love sinners but not their sin. Now we can compare unconditional love to unconditional acceptance.

As we mentioned when discussing Neo-Gnosticism theology, Neo-Gnostics believe in acceptance. They call it love, but they truly mean they want to accept everyone for almost anything. Due to their belief in subjective truth and ambiguity, they do not see a problem with accepting a person's lifestyle. We will call this unconditional acceptance.

---

37 "For many are called, but few are chosen." —Matthew 22:14 (ESV)

Neo-Gnostics believe that to truly love someone, they have to also accept the person's lifestyle. This is why things like the pride flag continually gain more and more colors. Each color represents a different sexual orientation or attraction. Every time one lifestyle becomes acceptable, another pops up and demands acceptance. This can also be seen in normal relationships. Dating has become a confusing web of sexual and non-sexual interactions that seem to have absolutely no rhyme or reason. People sleep around with who they want, how they want, and when they want. They also require everyone they meet to fully accept them, or they cannot be friends.

This is what is meant by unconditional acceptance. Accept me as I am now, never asking me to grow, change, or mature. They believe that they are perfectly fine as they are, and some even believe that they are perfect.[38]

This is not what God desires nor what Scripture teaches. As we have mentioned multiple times by this point, we are called to love but not always accept. We are called to grow and become more like Christ, not remain our broken evil selves. We are also called to help those around us, even if it is inconvenient. Christ was very inconvenienced when He came here to die.

Scripture uses an analogy that is very powerful. In Matthew 16:24,[39] Christ says that we need to deny or forget ourselves. The Greek word here is *aparneomai*. This means to deny, disown, repudiate, or disregard.[40] To love God, we need to deny ourselves to be with Him. This means that our fleshly de-

---

[38] Unfortunately, this is a growing belief. If mankind is good and it is only the environment that corrupts, then it is easy to conclude that mankind is also perfect.

[39] Then Jesus told his disciples, "If anyone would come after me, let him deny himself and take up his cross and follow me."

[40] "Strong's Greek: 533. ἀπαρνέομαι (Aparneomai) -- to Deny." *Biblehub.com*, biblehub.com/greek/533.htm.

sires, sins, and stubborn wants all need to be pushed aside to be with Him. When we are with Him, we are to love those around us. This means that to love our neighbors and our enemies, we have to deny ourselves as well. This can be as simple as denying ourselves a meal to give to someone hungry or can be as hard as moving to another country to share the gospel with the lost.

At the outset, this sounds like an impossible task. If we constantly deny ourselves, then we will live miserably and never amount to anything. But there are two counters to this. 1) We are never told we cannot also pursue earthly wants. We can pursue careers, families, and geographic locals. But we need to put Christ and His plans above our, and sometimes His plans will require us to love a person before ourselves, and His plans may require us to abandon some of our plans entirely. 2) God will support us and prosper us. Remember that verse we talked about a few chapters ago where Paul says he can do all things through Christ who strengthens him (Philippians 4:13)? This is where this verse applies. When we focus on Christ and His mission, God Himself will support us.[41] He will provide exactly what we need, and sometimes He gives us overwhelming abundance. Job, David, and Abraham are all examples of godly men who followed God first and were given everything anyone could think of. Abraham had so much wealth and power that neighboring kings treated him as an equal. When we follow God's plan, we can also be given the world. But that is never the point. Christ is the true blessing.

If He will cloth the lilies and feed the birds, why would He also not take care of His children? This is why we need to stop

---

41 "Look at the birds of the air: they neither sow nor reap nor gather into barns, and yet your heavenly Father feeds them. Are you not of more value than they? And which of you by being anxious can add a single hour to his span of life? And why are you anxious about clothing? Consider the lilies of the field, how they grow: they neither toil nor spin..." —Matthew 6:26–28 (ESV)

worrying about taking care of ourselves so much and worry about loving our neighbors and enemies. We have the Origin as our Provider; what else could we need?

Ending Remarks

When we look at love, we can see many different types. There is brotherly love (philia), there is erotic love (eros), and there is unconditional love (agapeo). When God speaks of love, at least concerning Himself and how we are to love, He uses the word *apageo*. This is because His love is always unconditional. We have done nothing to earn it, nor can we. We have absolutely no desire to be with Him until He turns our hearts around. Only then do we pursue Him.

God loved us so much that He was willing to come down and die for us even while we hated Him. That is love. Now He lives in our hearts, continually changing us to become more like Himself. He knew that we could not do it without Him, so He gave us a way. That is love.

Now He has commanded us to love those around us the way that He loved us. This is no easy task, but it is well worth it. We are to love the person with a selfless love because that is the only type of love. Selfish love is not love; it is selfishness. True love is only unconditional and selfless.

Loving Our Enemies

We are to love our neighbor and our enemy. Since Christ loved us while we were still enemies, we have no excuse for why we cannot love our enemies. This does not mean that we have to be best friends with them, but we do have to love them. Love shows a form of concern that can transcend any difference. This is why Christ used the example of the Good Samaritan. He loved his enemy even though he did not have to. He did not befriend him, he did not really associate with him after he was healed, but he gave him his time, his money, and his resources. That is love.

Love the Sinner, Not the Sin

We are to love the sinner, but we are never to love the sin. This is a difficult task, maybe more difficult than anything else mentioned in this chapter. There is no easy way to show a person that they are loved while not accepting their lifestyle. This does not have to be a verbal lifestyle condemnation. Christ did not have to tell the lady at the well that He did not agree with her lifestyle. There was no verbal condemnation. Most people who are living a life of sin know they are. They know they are doing something wrong. All we have to do is show them a loving alternative. If they accept Jesus, glory to God. If they do not, we can know that we did everything that we could. It was never in our hands to begin with. We were called to love and share the good news of Christ. We cannot change anyone.

Love Unconditional Like Christ

Love is not necessarily acceptance. They can, and usually are, two very different things. We are called to love people unconditionally. We are not called to accept everything a person does. There are many things that people do that are very damaging to themselves and to society. We have to unconditionally love like Christ did but not unconditionally accept their lifestyles. Cheap grace accepts everything; costly grace loves everything but requires everything to be reoriented toward the Origin, which is God.

Love is difficult. It requires perseverance, sacrifice, and change. It requires us to get over ourselves and to approach others in a way that is not in our nature. Unconditional love does not want something in return; it is not a transaction but a gift. This is what makes love so difficult and so foreign. We do not naturally love in an agapeo way. We put ourselves first, and whatever we have left over, we give to others, but that is not love. To truly understand what love is, we have to study Christ and everything He did. Only then can we truly understand what love is because He is the origin of love.

7

Serving

As we lose ourselves in the service of others, we discover our own lives and our own happiness.[1]

—Dieter F. Uchtdorf

What else is there on our journey now that we have discussed love? Is that not the ultimate goal of humanity? To reach a stage of perfect love? Obviously, based on the last chapter, that would be a no. Life's point should be understood by this point, but in case it is not, the point of our life is to serve God and enjoy Him forever.[2] Just like our last stop, this

[1] *Churchofjesuschrist.org*, 2022, abn.churchofjesuschrist.org/study/general-conference/2008/10/happiness-your-herit-age?lang=eng&adobe_mc_ref=https%3A%2F%2Fwww.churchofjesuschrist.org%2Fstudy%2Fgeneral-conference%2F2008%2F10%2Fhappiness-your-heritage%3Flang%3Deng&adobe_mc_sdid=SDID%3D6750C28C486B73A2-254672B7C9C40615%7CMCORGID%3D66C5485451E56AAE0A490D45%2540AdobeOrg%7CTS%3D1652062431. Accessed 9 May 2022.

[2] Anyone who has studied the Westminster Catechism knows this as the first catechism.

stop is also a controversial stop. How and who we serve is just as debated as how and who we love.

Do we serve everyone or selected individuals? Do we serve until we reach our limits, or do we continue? Are our enemies part of the list, or do we only serve friends or neutral individuals? The paths go on and on, making anyone's head spin. Why is life so difficult? Is there anything in this world simple?

The answer to these last two questions is, in fact, simple. Life is simple when we follow the Author and Origin of it all, who is God. When we follow our own paths, life becomes a wreck. The subject of this chapter is exactly the same. When we look to our Origin, we can learn how and who to serve. When we look to our own selves, we wander in the desolation of our own wisdom.

Why Serve

The first important thing about serving is that it stems from love. Once we understand the unconditional love that Christ had for us, it is much easier to pour that love back out onto the world. Just like how Christ came to serve the world, we also are called to serve everyone. Scripture gives many reasons why we should serve and many examples to show how. The form of serving being mentioned here is working for others. Christ loved us through His actions, and we need to follow His example.

Clearly, the prime example of serving is Christ. He did not come to lord over us as many religious leaders did but, in fact, to do the opposite. This is clear when reading any gospel. The main point of Jesus was to save us from our sins, but he also came to be an example of how to live. He showed us that we need to love those around us by serving them.

One reason why we need to discuss serving is that it has become a very convoluted subject. Many Neo-Gnostics, as we have discussed, do not serve others much. Like all humans, they will serve themselves all day long. But when it comes to taking an extended amount of time, money, or any other resource for others, they come up very short.

The concept of *self-love* has removed service from being a primary characteristic of a good person. Though, to be fair, many Christians have reduced their charitable acts to a minimum as well. This has been very distressing to our culture. Many Christians live for Christ on Sunday and Wednesday (the two main days Christians go to church) but rarely take Him with them any other day of the week.

With that said, Christians are still much more likely to contribute to charitable causes than non-religious individuals.[3] Though to be clear, the study here mentions religious individuals in general. Either way, this study excludes Neo-Gnostics. At best, they are loose participants in religious communities and, at worst, wholly against them. This puts them, more often than not, in non-religious groups. As we have mentioned in previous chapters, Neo-Gnostics dislike church, Scripture, and Christ being the only path. Because of these views, it is safe to claim that most Neo-Gnostics are spiritual deists of some form.

Another reason why this is an important topic is that Neo-Gnostics do not believe that it is important to share the gospel. This is because for Neo-Gnostics, Christianity is no different than any other religion. Since they believe that we can reach heaven through any path, it does not matter that the gospel is shared.

For Christians, there are two forms of serving. First, there is the physical type, which is where all of the usual forms of service happen. Second, there is spiritual service. Most people,

---

[3] https://www.washingtontimes.com. *The Washington Times*. "Religious People More Likely to Give to Charity, Study Shows." The Washington Times, www.washingtontimes.com/news/2017/oct/30/religious-people-more-likely-give-charity-study/#:~:text=On%20average%2C%20religiously%20affiliated%20households%20donate%20%241%2C590%20to. Accessed 26 Sept. 2021.

whether theistic or atheistic, believe that physical service is important. Helping the poor, building homes for the needy, making water sources for the thirsty, or adopting orphans are all universal examples of understood good.[4]

The real difference happens when we start to serve the spiritual needs of others. Many individuals do not believe that the spiritual side of life is very important. Neo-Gnostics will speak heavily about mental and emotional health, but when it comes to spiritual health, they are silent.

The most popular example of spiritual service is when Christians share the gospel. This is a primary goal for us because it was one of the two commands given by Christ before His ascension. We are to spread His good news to anyone, anywhere. The issue is that since Neo-Gnostics do not believe that Christ is the only way to heaven, they do not see any point in sharing His good news. Also, since they do not believe in objective truth, they do not believe that one person should discuss their truth with another person in the hopes that they will change their mind. This means that a Neo-Gnostic will never try to "convert" a person to Christianity because they do not fully believe that Christianity is special or worth it.[5]

It seems that most Neo-Gnostics do not fully understand the significance of physical and spiritual service. If we truly love someone, we should want to save their physical bodies as well as their souls. Also, if we truly believe that Christ is the only way to salvation and heaven, then we should feel a strong compulsion to tell people.

---

[4] The sad part is that while everyone will state these as good things, so many people will never act to help.

[5] Convert is in quotes because we do not convert. The Holy Spirit breaks the heart of stone and makes it beat again. What our actual part is in this process is unknow. We only know that we are called to share the gospel. Our talking does not take away or add anything to the Spirit's work.

Healing Physical and Spiritual Needs

There are many examples of Christ serving while He was ministering. Numerous passages in Scripture show Christ healing both physical ailments and spiritual issues. He does this because he loves His people, and he wants to show that love. People would travel from far and wide to hear Him teach and to be healed.[6]

In Matthew 9:35, we see the two most important activities that Christ did during His ministry. Outside of His death and resurrection, of course. He preached the gospel and healed the sick. This shows that we are to spread the good news, and we are to serve those around us. Christ was demonstrating that He cared for both the spiritual well-being of His creation and their physical well-being. He did not just make this world to only save the spiritual. God desires for us to minister to both needs. We cannot abandon one without abandoning the other.

Outside of following Christ's example, there are two other reasons why we should be drawn to ministering to the soul and the body. 1) We have been saved by Christ, and that should produce a desire to pass on that love. 2) We are commanded by Christ to spread the gospel and to love our neighbor. Since we are to live in simple obedience, this is a command that we cannot ignore.

Serve Because Christ Served Us

This reason is simple. Christ saved us from eternal damnation, and we should be filled with a sense of love and gratitude that compels us to share with others so that they can experience the same thing. We know what life is like without the love and

---

[6] "And Jesus went throughout all the cities and villages, teaching in their synagogues and proclaiming the gospel of the kingdom and healing every disease and every affliction." —Matthew 9:35 (ESV)

hope of Christ, and we want others to experience what we have in Christ.

This is not an obligation. Here we do not share because we must. God is not forcing us to tell people begrudgingly about His grace and salvation. This desire is a product of what salvation and grace do. We are no longer shackled to the repetitious evils of this world. We have been freed, and we want to go free others with the same truth.

The way we feel can be compared to the feeling of finding a new service that saves either time or money. A new phone company is a good example in our technologically filled lives. In our modern world, everyone must have a phone. They are practically a necessity. We navigate with them, communicate with them, are entertained with them, and they are our alarms and calendars. When our phone breaks or gets lost, it feels like our world has ended.[7] But the downside is their cost. Cellular service can be expensive. So, when we stumble upon a new service that saves us money while giving a similar or better service, we go nuts. We go and tell everyone about it. We suddenly become a free commercial for them. We tell people about their plans, phone payments, and every positive thing possible. This is done because we honestly love our experience, and we want our friends and family to experience the same thing.

The gospel is the same, just on a much larger scale. When we experience God and realize exactly what He has done for us and how much he has saved us, we cannot do anything but tell everyone we meet. The gospel tells us that since we are naturally sinners, God had to do something to bring us back into contact with Himself.[8]

---

[7] A little bit dramatic, but still true

[8] "He himself bore our sins in his body on the tree, that we might die to sin and live to righteousness. By his wounds you have been healed." —1 Peter 2:24 (ESV)

God is pure and holy, meaning that He cannot come into contact with sin. Not that it would damage Him, but that He would destroy the sin and the sinner along with it. Because God loves us, He decided to come and die in our place. Christ came and took our place so that now we can stand before God without His holiness destroying us.[9] Christ came down and lived a perfect life, but He still had to die one of the most painful deaths possible. He was flogged, beaten, stuck by a crown of thorns, and hung on a cross. He did all of this just so that we could be with Him again. Unconditional love produces a heart of unconditional sacrifice.

Before, we were slaves to sin, forced by our own corruption to choose the wrong path over and over again, but now we have been bought by Christ's blood, making us free and able to choose the correct path—the path to life, hope, and love. This is the most magnificent piece of news a person will ever receive.

Slave To Sin or Christ?

But what does it mean to be a slave to sin or to Christ? First, Slavery in the ancient Roman empire was very different than how we view slavery today. We see slavery through the lens of the post-scientific revolution. Since then, slavery has gone through a dramatic shift. In ancient times people became slaves due to a debt or war. The concept of racial differences was drastically different than it is today. Of course, there were ethnic and cultural differences, but the concept of race as we understand it did not exist.

When one group conquered another, it was common for the victor to take slaves. This was done for multiple reasons. First, to remove some of the population and transplant them

[9] This is like when gold is put into a fire—it removes all of the blemishes. The blemishes cannot stand in the presence of the fire because the fire devours them, not that the blemishes damage the flame.

across the growing empire. Second, the victor wanted the strongest or prettiest to increase the status of their empire.[10] Lastly, most empires needed cheap expendable labor, and a newly conquered people were perfect for the job.

The other common way to become a slave was debt. Usually, when an individual owed a person a significant amount of money, they would become an indentured servant for a certain number of years. After their debt was paid, they were free again. Though, an interesting thing about this form of slavery was that some individuals chose to continue serving a family instead of going free because they lived a better life with them than in freedom.

When Paul speaks on slavery in Romans 6:20–23,[11] he says that we were slaves to sin and that sin was our master. Because sin was our master, we followed its every command. In most cases, we even enjoyed it. We developed a liking for the evilness that Satan has to offer.

But God set us free. For a slave to have their debt paid, they have to have a benefactor or their debt worked off. Unfortunately for us, our debt keeps growing because we continually sin. For argument's sake, every time we work off one sin, we have replaced it with five. God knew that we could never pay Him back. This is why He stepped in and paid the ultimate price for us.

Because of the sacrifice of Christ, we have now been bought by a new master. This master is kind and loving, unlike

---

10 This is why Daniel and his friends were taken after Babylon conquered them.

11 "For when you were slaves of sin, you were free in regard to righteousness. But what fruit were you getting at that time from the things of which you are now ashamed? For the end of those things is death. But now that you have been set free from sin and have become slaves of God, the fruit you get leads to sanctification and its end, eternal life. For the wages of sin is death, but the free gift of God is eternal life in Christ Jesus our Lord." — Romans 6:20–23 (ESV)

our last master, who was sin, and He desires for us to be free. Not only does He want us to be free, as if that was not enough, but He also wants to adopt us into His family. In Ephesians 1:5 (ESV), Paul writes, "he predestined us for adoption to himself as sons through Jesus Christ, according to the purpose of his will."

So not only have we been freed from a cruel master, but we have also now been adopted by a kind, loving father who is adding us to His will. There can be no better event in life than this. This is the act that should motivate us to spread the gospel. We should be so happy about our circumstances that we should want to share it with every person we know. To use the phrase, we should want to "shout it from the rooftops."

Now that we are freed, it should be our desire to free others. This abolition comes in two waves. The first wave is spiritual, while the second is physical. First, we desire to free other prisoners from the impound of Lucifer. For some, this can be a long, arduous task since we enjoy our sin and desire to bathe in its lusts. But we cannot convince anyone on our own to leave this pool; only God can show someone what true light looks like. What we do is plant the seeds and let the Holy Spirit do the watering.

This is where the second task comes into play. While we minister to the soul,[12] we can minister to the body. God desires us to heal the sick and tend to the wounded. By doing this, we can show how we are different and what God has done for us. As usual, we can go to the Scripture to see how God wants us to minister to the physical needs of those around us.

We do not have to go into too much detail here since we already saw in quite a bit of depth in the last chapter how to love someone. Here, loving and serving are identical. But there is one thing that needs to be mentioned. That is to caution against too much religious study. This statement might come as a shock

---

[12] Planting seeds

to some due to what we have been discussing so far in this book. We should never stop studying Scripture, but the issue comes when studying becomes our start, middle, and end, and serving fades into the distance.

This is what the religious elites did[13] in Jesus's day. This is what the religious men did in the parable of the Good Samaritan. They were too busy reading and "serving" God that they had no time to serve their fellow man. They were too busy loving religion to love their neighbor. Bonhoeffer wrote, in *Life Together*,

> We must be ready to allow ourselves to be interrupted by God … We may pass them by, preoccupied with our more important tasks, as the priest passed by the man who had fallen among thieves, perhaps reading the Bible.[14]

What Bonhoeffer is saying is that if we focus on too much intellectual study and too little on service, we miss the point of the gospel. The story of the Good Samaritan, which he is referring to, is about simple action and obedience.

Works not Works

We must stop for a second and discuss the concept of works. This does lead us to a controversial topic. God calls us to do works,[15] but we have to be sure that we are not pursuing them for salvation. Salvation is through faith; faith produces works (works is another word for service or charity). We have been

---

[13] And do

[14] Dietrich Bonhoeffer, et al. *Life Together*. Minneapolis, Fortress Press, 2015, p. 99.

[15] Service

saved by the works of one man: Jesus Christ. No one else's works can save their soul.

This concept of works can be seen in James 2:14–18.[16] James is saying that faith in Christ may be enough to get into the kingdom of heaven, but if a brother or sister does not have works, it is a strong testament that their faith is not real. We cannot be the judge of whether a person is saved. But a changed heart will produce changed actions. If a life is lived exactly as it had been before, then it is hard to believe that a true understanding of Christ has occurred. As mentioned above, if we truly understand the redemption and sacrifice of Christ, we will be radically changed.

One misinterpretation of James' words is that works save. This is not true. It is not the works that save us, but the fact that works prove our faith. Only one man's works had the power to save; for the rest of us, we use our works as an outpouring of love for that one act. Mark makes the point by telling the story of Christ and the fig tree.

> On the following day, when they came from Bethany, he was hungry. And seeing in the distance a fig tree in leaf, he went to see if he could find anything on it. When he came to it, he found nothing but leaves, for it was not the season for figs. And he said to it, "May no one ever eat fruit from you again." And his disciples heard it. (Mark 11:12–14 ESV)

---

16 "What good is it, my brothers, if someone says he has faith but does not have works? Can that faith save him? If a brother or sister is poorly clothed and lacking in daily food, and one of you says to them, 'Go in peace, be warmed and filled,' without giving them the things needed for the body, what good is that? So also faith by itself, if it does not have works, is dead. But someone will say, 'You have faith and I have works.' Show me your faith apart from your works, and I will show you my faith by my works." —James 2:14–18 (ESV)

This story is often misunderstood. Jesus was not mad at a tree because it did not have any fruit, and He was hungry. He knew when fig trees were in season and when they were not. To understand this story, we must go beneath the surface. Christ was telling His disciples that a tree with no fruit is useless. The tree may be there, it may be absorbing sunlight, and it may look nice, but its job is not being fulfilled.

We are like a fig tree. We are planted in our communities just like a tree. Our roots spread out, and we produce branches and leaves. This is where the analogy turns a little dark. Our season in life and what nutrients we absorb dictate what type of fruit we produce or if we produce at all. If we absorb too much corrupting nutrients, we will spiritually die. Death does not produce fruit. A fig tree without figs is pointless. A Christian without works is dead. Just like James, Jesus shows that a fruitless life is dead.

Sin Is Sin

We need to take a second and restate that all sins are considered the same to God. We forget that all sins lead to eternal death and separation from God. God does not differentiate between theft, adultery, homosexuality, and murder. From His point of view, they are all worthy of damnation. Viewing sin as better or worse is an issue for two reasons. First, we start to develop an incorrect point system with some believers being better than others, and second, we decline to love and serve others because we believe that their sin is too bad.

This is common when it comes to sexual sin. Adultery and pornography have become rampant, and we seem to be fine with that fact. We intellectually know that God hates sexual sin of any kind, but we explain away these sins. We say that our situation is different or that sin is actually not that bad. We rationalize our sin in our own heads to make it seem insignificant.

26% to 34%[17] of Christians have been divorced, but divorce has become all too comfortable for Christians.[18] We come up with a myriad of reasons to excuse the behavior. But besides the two reasons God prescribed (death and infidelity),[19] it is a sin. Likewise, about 64% of men watch porn on some type of regular basis. Pornography is even rising among women, with more and more women watching it at least once a month.[20] That is a lot of young people lusting after men and women who are not their married partners. As sins become normalized, we view them as tolerable sins. We claim that while they may be bad, they are not as bad as this sin or that sin.

A popular sin that Christians like to focus on, at least at the moment, is homosexuality. While this is a sin, it is no better or worse than the two mentioned above (adultery and pornography). We try to excuse our sins in our heads by pointing fingers at a sin perceived to be worse. Christ had some specific words on this matter.

> Why do you see the speck that is in your brother's eye, but do not notice the log that is in your own eye? Or how can you say to your brother, 'Let me take the speck out of your eye,' when there is the log in your own eye? You hypocrite, first take the log out of your own eye, and then you will see clearly to take the speck out of your brother's eye. (Matt. 7:3–5 ESV)

---

[17] Admin. "Christian Divorce Rate - Divorce - LAWS.com." *Divorce,* 3 Apr. 2015, divorce.laws.com/christian-divorce-rate.

[18] The difference depends on the denomination and religious conviction.

[19] Matthew 5:32, Mark 10:11–12, Luke 16:18, and I Corinthians 7:39

[20] Ltd, Proven Men Ministries. "2014 Survey: How Many Christians Do You Think Watch Porn?" *www.prnewswire.com,* www.prnewswire.com/news-releases/2014-survey-how-many-christians-do-you-think-watch-porn-271236741.html. Accessed 27 Sept. 2021.

On a side note, this is proof that Christ could be sarcastic. Christ is asking why we focus on our brother's problems when we have our own issues to deal with. We need to deal with our own issues before we start pointing at another's. This statement is slightly sarcastic because it is impossible for us to fix our problems. If someone has a plank in their eye, they are in need of drastic surgery. That is why He came down to earth in the first place. Christ is the surgeon, and only He can fix our problems. Christ is saying that we need to focus on Him, and He will fix our sins, just like our brothers and sisters will look to Him to fix theirs.

This issue goes back to how we serve our brothers and sisters. Bonhoeffer writes again in *Life Together*, "How can I possibly serve another person in unfeigned humility if I seriously regard his sinfulness as worse than my own?"[21] When we think that our sin is not as bad as another's, we not only cannot serve them, but we are also spitting on the works that Christ did. Unlike the Rabbi, the Samaritan did not regard himself better than the hurt man. If he did, he would not have helped him. He saw him as a fellow human being who needed help. He knew that it was his duty as a worshiper of God to help those in need.

If we correctly understand Christ's sacrifice, we will develop humility. When we realize that we did nothing to deserve our salvation, we cannot hold ourselves above anyone. We believe in salvation by grace, not works. Meaning that it was only by the desire and will of God that we are saved. This makes humility an unavoidable side-product of salvation. Once we have been given humility, we will naturally lean toward the attitude of service. When we understand what has been done for us and that we have very little to do with our salvation, humility is a byproduct. It is hard to be prideful when we are

---

[21] Dietrich Bonhoeffer, et al. *Life Together*. Minneapolis, Fortress Press, 2015, p. 97.

completely grateful to God. True service requires humility. Prideful individuals do not serve people.

I Command You to Serve

Though we are to serve joyfully, out of a heart of love and thankfulness, we are also told to serve. We are even told that God has laid aside works for us.[22]

If we are truly saved, then God has set aside specific works for us. These tasks are specially made to fit us and our unique qualifications. These acts of service are not chores, nor are they supposed to be a drudge. God has given us works that will fulfill us more than anything that we could choose. And as we have discussed before, even if they are difficult jobs, God will provide the strength (Philippians 4:13).

Christ first followed this command which means that we have no excuse not to do it. He, being a perfect leader, did not command us to serve while not serving Himself. Since He was commanding us to serve, He wanted to show that He was willing to serve in the most humiliating way. Jesus was God and the savior of the world, but He still put on the outfit of a slave and washed His disciple's feet. This story is found in John 13:3–5 and 12–17.[23]

---

22 "For we are his workmanship, created in Christ Jesus for good works, which God prepared beforehand, that we should walk in them." — Ephesians 2:10 (ESV)

23 "Jesus, knowing that the Father had given all things into his hands, and that he had come from God and was going back to God, rose from supper. He laid aside his outer garments, and taking a towel, tied it around his waist. Then he poured water into a basin and began to wash the disciples' feet and to wipe them with the towel that was wrapped around him … When he had washed their feet and put on his outer garments and resumed his place, he said to them, 'Do you understand what I have done to you? You call me Teacher and Lord, and you are right, for so I am. If I then, your Lord and Teacher, have washed your feet, you also ought to wash one another's feet. For I have given you an example, that you also should do just

This was a radical moment both back then as well as for today. Jesus, God, the savior of mankind, stooped down and did the job of the lowliest of servants. Rulers did not lower themselves to the status of a slave, but Christ did. He not only shows them how they are supposed to act, but He also states it in as clear of terms as possible. He tells them to serve each other. He even adds to that by showing that we are to serve in a way of perceived humiliation. He would have been ridiculed by the religious leaders of that day and of today for doing what He did. But again, Christ was showing that we were to serve anyone, and no job is too low.

If no man is greater than another, then we cannot claim to be better than anyone. Therefore, we can serve without any perceived social humiliation because we are all equal. This is one of the most radical statements and actions of Christianity. This aspect alone is what disrupted Medieval society and started the egalitarian movement of the Enlightenment.

The last part of this passage is that Christ knew where He came from and where He was going. We have this information as well. We came from God, and we are going back to God. This form of acceptance and contentment, which we now have because of Christ, also allows us to act in humble servitude. When we are no longer ignorant of our beginning nor of our end, we receive a peace that transcends pride, humiliation, or apathy.

Now we can serve because 1) Christ served first, 2) we came from God and are going back to God, and 3) we are all equals.

---

as I have done to you. Truly, truly, I say to you, a servant is not greater than his master, nor is a messenger greater than the one who sent him. If you know these things, blessed are you if you do them.'" —John 13:3–5; 12–17 (ESV)

Ending Remarks

When we go through life, we have two choices we can make when it comes to our neighbors. The first choice is to serve and love them. The second is to serve and love ourselves. Christ taught the first method, but the world loves the second. Neo-Gnostics love the second because they practice self-love. It is hard to serve others when we are focusing on ourselves.

Christ showed us that the first form of love is an unconditional, sacrificial love. It requires us to put others before ourselves. This is a hard thing to do. We have desires, both great and small, that we want to accomplish. Sometimes these desires are as small as sitting on a couch after a long day's work. But as we drive home, we see a person with a flat tire on the side of the road. We have two choices at that moment. Either we can follow Christ and sacrifice our desires for relaxation by helping the person, or we can follow our desires and leave the person to fend for themselves.

Scripture teaches us to follow Christ's sacrificial path. But our modern culture says more and more to fend for ourselves and leave the rest to do the same. Neo-Gnostics tend to follow the example of the culture, not of Christ. The modern focus on *self-love* and extreme mental health care has caused people to forsake their fellow man and focus on making sure they are safe first. Mental health is very important. But it seems like more and more people have developed crippling mental health issues. We, as a society, have become mental health hypochondriacs. There are those who actually suffer from depression or anxiety, but there are a lot of people who use mental health as an excuse not to have to help others. All too often, Neo-Gnostics claim that they cannot do something because they have reached their limit and they have to take care of themselves for a while.

We all need to make sure that we are healthy and not overextending ourselves. But this is very different than how Neo-Gnostics mean it. Scripture's example shows that through

Christ's strength, we can serve longer and harder than ever perceived possible (Philippians 4:13). Those who serve through this strength and through His wisdom rarely tire.

To use the flat tire analogy again, we can stop and help replace the tire even though we are already tired because it is not for ourselves or by ourselves. Service is being done for someone else, by someone else's strength. Changing a tire can be a hard, dirty job. It requires getting on the ground, grabbing objects that have been driving over all kinds of terrain, and replacing them with something that has been in storage for months or even years. But serving is a blessing that we can give to others because we have been given the best service possible, Christ's payment. This can also be a blessing to someone having a bad day. Since we do not know what is going on in another's life, we should serve so that they might see Christ.

Since we have been gifted Christ's sacrifice, we are able to gift others our time and resources. Since we are commanded to serve, we can follow that command and Christ's example and love those around us.

Service can be one of the most satisfying actions we can ever do. It is hard, tiring, and it requires us to sacrifice our time, money, or resources. But we will never regret serving someone. Christ first served us, so we can serve Him.

SECTION III

8

Covenants

For this is my blood of the covenant, which is poured out for many for the forgiveness of sins.

—Matthew 26:28 ESV

As our journey has progressed, there has been a cliff slowly drawing closer and closer. Up until this point, it was not much to mention, but now it is directly in front of us. The interesting thing about the cliff face is that there is a lit cave that our path is heading directly toward. As we approach the mouth, we see a carved tapestry covering the walls. The first clear thing is some wording that reads "the covenants of God. Look, all are welcome."

This chapter and the next will be a little different compared to the rest of the book. Before, we were looking at topics that have been debated over the years. We were arguing through different topics and seeing why the Neo-Gnostics have a faulty belief system. So far, we have seen that out of the two, traditional Christianity is far superior logically and morally to its progressive counterpart.

Here we are going to discuss some of the differences that make Christianity stand out as a religion in general, while still focusing on Neo-Gnosticism specifically. One argument by many out there today is that Christianity is no different than any other religion, and thus it can be lumped in with the masses. This is not true, and we are going to first look at the promises that God made to mankind to show why.[1]

God's Love For Us in Covenants

Christianity is very unique in the fact that our God desires to know us intimately. Most gods in other religions only care to know a few mortals, if any, and those mortals were usually men or women of great renown. To get the attention of a god, an individual had to be great themselves. Our God, on the other hand, does not require us to be great. Usually, He pursues individuals who we would consider ordinary or even insignificant.[2]

This puts us in a very different sphere compared to other religions. Instead of trying to please an angry, lustful, or drunken god,[3] we are trying to please our heavenly Father[4] because we desire His love and devotion.

Outside of us wanting to please Him, He has made contracts with us to show that He is going to love, protect, and bless us. These formal promises are unlike any other religious promise. They are also important for multiple reasons.

First, we need to know that we can trust God. Our souls are completely in His hands. If He were not trustworthy, then we would be making a grave error. An untrustworthy god is no better than an untrustworthy person. In fact, the god would probably be worse. Covenants (an unchangeable divinely im-

---

[1] To be fair, no religion is the same. Even polytheistic religions differ from each other.

[2] Luckily God does not focus on the things this world focuses on.

[3] As many of the Greek gods tend to be portrayed

[4] 2 Corinthians 6:18

posed legal agreement between God and man that stipulates the conditions of their relationship[5]) have two components: earthy and heavenly. God made earthly promises to mankind to show that He always keeps his promises. The heavenly parts are for salvation.

Secondly, covenants help us understand the relationship God desires. He desires to be intimate, but sin has driven a schism between us. Throughout history, God has been righting that schism. To God, it was a quick process. To us, it took thousands of years. Because of this, God made covenants with us to let us know what He is planning.

The last reason is to help us understand salvation and the path God took to save us. History can be seen as a slow crawl toward salvation. Each piece fits into the overall master plan set up by God. Scripture helps us put those pieces together. The covenants are the promises that God made, setting up the field for Christ.

Our mission is to make disciples of all people. As we discussed in the last chapter, we do this because we truly believe that a relationship with God is the one and only way to have meaning in this life. But we cannot carry out this command if we do not understand the relationship that we have. The gospel is the most important message anyone can share or hear, but its impact is lost if the believer cannot explain why this gift is unique and amazing. If we cannot explain the difference between Christianity and other religions, then our mission is doomed to fail.

Specific Relationships with God

Neo-Gnostics claim that all religions are similar enough that one path will lead to the same conclusion as another. This we

[5] Grudem, Wayne A. *Making Sense of Series: One of Seven Parts from Grudem's Systematic Theology*. Grand Rapids, Mi, Zondervan, 1994, p. 515.

discussed in the first section. We discussed how Neo-Gnostics believe that they have a special relationship with God. But how can they claim to have a special agreement with God when the only agreements that he has made with man were concerning the Jews or salvation? This is where this type of belief becomes difficult to defend. Neo-Gnostics like to bring up their relationship when they do not want to follow specific parts of Scripture. But God only enters these types of relationships with specific people, at specific times in history, for one specific reason.

There is one simple reason why God has entered into any special relationship, and that is Christ. Christ is the central reason for every aspect of Scripture. Everything God includes in Scripture points to Christ and His salvational impact on the world.

What Is a Covenant?

Before we can begin discussing the promises that God made to mankind, we have to define the term "covenant." A good definition is by Wayne Grudem's *Systematic Theology*, which defines a covenant as such: "A covenant is an unchangeable divinely imposed legal agreement between God and man that stipulates the conditions of their relationship."[6]

Most covenants contain two parts. First, they have an earthly component. This part illustrated that God was able to do what He said He was going to do. The second part deals with Christ and salvation. All of Scripture leads to one thing: Christ. Every covenant either directly or indirectly points to Christ.[7]

---

[6] Grudem, Wayne A. *Making Sense of Series: One of Seven Parts from Grudem's Systematic Theology*. Grand Rapids, Mi, Zondervan, 1994, p. 515.

[7] There is no other reason for Scripture. It is not a good moral, philosophical book to be set next to Plato, Newton, and Kant. Scripture, as we have dis-

In total, God entered into seven different covenants at seven different times. These covenants come in a few different forms. Firstly, there are the unilateral, unconditional, or one-sided promises. This means that only one party needs to uphold their end of the bargain to keep the covenant active. The second is bilateral, conditional, or two-sided. This requires both parties to uphold the agreement; otherwise, the covenant is broken.

Most of the covenants written in the Bible are between Israel and God and are unilateral. These are the promises of land, prosperity, and salvation that God made with His chosen people. God made promises with Adam, Abraham, Noah, Moses, the Israelites, David, and all of mankind. Each covenant is unique and gives us different glimpses into the character of God and His relationship with His creation.

Covenants Between God and People

In Greek, the common term for agreements was *syntheke*. This was used when both sides were equal, and the covenant could be broken by either side.[8] Instead, the New Testament authors used the word *diatheke*.[9] This means that the agreement was going to be produced by only one side. This was most commonly used for wills or final testaments.

This distinction is important because it shows that God never intended us to be liable for the fulfillment of the promis-

---

cussed, is truth.

8 "Gamblers Anonymous." *The Compass*, 26 Feb. 2011, www.thecompassnews.org/2011/02/why-we-call-them-testaments-and-not-wills/. Accessed 9 May 2022.

9 "Strong's Greek: 1242. διαθήκη (Diathéké) -- Testament, Will, Covenant." *Biblehub.com*, 2022, biblehub.com/greek/1242.htm. Accessed 9 May 2022.

es. The authors knew this and made it clear that only God instituted the covenants, and only He can sustain them.

In the Old Testament, the word used for covenant is *berith*.[10] This was the Hebrew equivalent to *syntheke*. While the word was used more as an agreement between equal parties, God shows that His covenants are between unequal parties by His actions. We will go over this concept in more detail later, but for now, we can just say that ancient Middle Eastern cultures had their own way of making covenants and differentiating between unilateral and bilateral agreements.

Adamic Covenant

The first covenant was made between God and Adam. Obviously, Adam being the first man, God made His first covenant with him. This covenant was made after creation and ended when Adam and Eve sinned, which is when God promised them salvation.

After God created man on the sixth day, He gave him one commandment.

> The LORD God took the man and put him in the garden of Eden to work it and keep it. And the LORD God commanded the man, saying, "You may surely eat of every tree of the garden, but of the tree of the knowledge of good and evil you shall not eat, for in the day that you eat of it you shall surely die." (Gen. 2:15–17 ESV)

This covenant is a bilateral agreement. As stated in the passage, God blessed Adam and Eve with Eden. Adam is Hebrew

[10] "Strong's Hebrew: 1285. בְּרִית (Berith) -- Covenant." *Biblehub.com*, 2022, biblehub.com/hebrew/1285.htm. Accessed 9 May 2022.

for "man."[11] Eve means "life" in Hebrew.[12] But there was a requirement to keep these benefits. They had to not eat of the tree of knowledge of good and evil. The punishment for breaking this command would not only be losing the blessings but that Adam and Eve would also die.

We see that this death was not only physical but also spiritual.[13] Their death was literal, though not immediate, but what they did not know was that their sin caused a separation between man and God. God could no longer walk with them because there was now a rift torn between the holy God and unholy man.

This rift was allowed because God made Adam and Eve with a free will, and they chose to disobey the one command that God had given them.[14] Adam and Eve were allowed the choice to either eat the fruit or not. They chose to disobey God, thus corrupting themselves. Because of this breach of the covenant, God cast them out of the garden. Before removing them

---

11 Campbell, Mike. "Meaning, Origin and History of the Name Adam." *Behind the Name*, 2020, www.behindthename.com/name/adam. Accessed 9 May 2022.

12 "Strong's Hebrew: 2332. חַוָּה (Chavvah) -- "Life," the First Woman." *Biblehub.com*, 2022, biblehub.com/hebrew/2332.htm. Accessed 9 May 2022.

13 Though there is a debate on whether the death was only spiritual or both spiritual and physical.

14 This brings up the eternal debate between free will and determinism. Both must be true for God and salvation to be true. Without free will we are robots and sin cannot be because it would be God's fault that we sinned because He would have caused us to sin. Also, determinism has to be true otherwise God would not be omniscient (all-knowing) or omnipotent (all-powerful). If we had the ability to choose salvation without God, then Christ would not be needed. Also, if we could choose salvation without God knowing, then He obviously is not omniscient nor omnipotent, thus nullifying Him as God. There either would be a being stronger than He or no God at all.

from paradise, God gives them the first hint of His plan for salvation.

This is the first reference to the final covenant made by God through Christ.[15] The mention of the offspring of the woman is Christ. Lucifer tried to kill Christ; this is the bruising of the heel. But Christ would vanquish death; this is the bruising of the head. On the day of Christ's crucifixion, Lucifer thought he had beat God, but Christ rose on the third day, paying the cost for sin. This is also in reference to Lucifer trying to destroy man since man is God's precious creation. Lucifer hates mankind and desires to make us miserable. While he succeeds in making us miserable, he will never truly end us, which is his second greatest failure. The first is his defeat by Christ on the cross.

Need for the Second Adam

Because all mankind is descended from Adam, we are all under the curse of sin. This is why we need a second Adam. Scripture tells us that this second Adam would come and live the perfect life that Adam was supposed to live. This second Adam is Christ.[16]

The Adamic covenant dispels the notion of man's goodness. It is common among Neo-Gnostics to believe that mankind is naturally good. But it is impossible to believe in our natural goodness when Adam and Eve, living in perfection, erred. If they could not follow one command, how can we follow the multitudes required in today's world? It is lunacy to believe in inherent goodness based on the first three chapters of Genesis alone. We were made perfect, placed in paradise, and we still chose to follow our own desires. The Adamic covenant shows us our pension to err and God's desire to redeem us.

---

[15] Genesis 3:15

[16] I Corinthians 15:45–49

Noahic Covenant

Many centuries after Adam came Noah. Noah lived at the antediluvian peak of debauchery. We are told in the verses leading up to the flood (starting in Genesis 5) that mankind had grown in their evil. We are not told any specifics in chapter six except that their hearts and minds only focused on evil. This was when God flooded the earth, destroying all of mankind but Noah, his wife, his three sons, and their wives. When the waters went down after forty days and forty nights, the ark rested on Mount Ararat. Noah made an offering to God, and this is when God made His covenant with Noah that He would never again destroy the world by water.

> Then God said to Noah and to his sons with him, "Behold, I establish my covenant with you and your offspring after you, and with every living creature that is with you, the birds, the livestock, and every beast of the earth with you, as many as came out of the ark; it is for every beast of the earth. I establish my covenant with you, that never again shall all flesh be cut off by the waters of the flood, and never again shall there be a flood to destroy the earth." (Gen. 9:8–11 ESV)

An interesting aspect of this first true covenant (the Adamic covenant may be a covenant, but it is not a formal covenant between God and man like the other six covenants) is that it is made with all of creation, not just mankind. Another major aspect of this covenant is that it shows God's love for His creation. This love is not just a spiritual love but also physical. Many Gnostics believed that the physical world was evil, but the fact that God saved animals by placing them on the Ark disproves this belief. God would not save things that He did not care for. God must care for the physical form of His creation if He would take the time to specifically tell Noah how to save them.

Scripture says that it is for the sake of every beast that He made the covenant with Noah. This tells us that God cared for His whole creation. Not just the spiritual world, not just mankind, but the whole physical world.

The Gnostics followed a belief called dualism. This meant that life was split into the spiritual and the material. They believed that creation and the fall happened at the same time. The belief is that when the soul became trapped in the material flesh, it became sinful. Sin is not a disagreeing with God's commands, but it is a misunderstanding of our true nature. This lack of knowledge causes us to act in the wrong way.[17]

Neo-Gnostics have taken the opposite route and believe that nature is pure and that mankind needs to reconnect with their primal selves to save not only nature[18] but ourselves as well. While the outward expression may be different, the inward beliefs are still the same. It is clear that Neo-Gnostics care for this world greatly. This is good because we are called to be stewards of our planet. The issue lies at the heart of the matter, or literally the heart.

Along with believing that the material is good comes the belief that the heart is good. Neo-Gnostics believe that man is inherently good and only lacks a correct environment to flourish in. This thought was popularized by the French philosopher Rousseau in the eighteenth century. This belief can only be held if Scripture is held second. God clearly states that man is full of evil. He declares that it is the heart of man that is evil, not their environment or society.[19]

---

[17] gnosticismexplained.org/anticosmicism-gnostic-dualism/

[18] Due to climate change

[19] Cameron, Janet. "Jean-Jacques Rousseau – We Are Good by Nature but Corrupted by Society»." *Decodedpast.com*, 25 Nov. 2013, decodedpast.com/jean-jacques-rousseau-we-are-good-by-nature-but-corrupted-by-society/. Ac-

This is where the great lie of inherent good resides. If nature, including man, is naturally good, then all we have to do is figure out what is the most natural way of being. Once this is discovered, then life will be at peace. The problem with this theory is that Scripture, science, and psychology disagree with it.

We have already discussed scripturally how mankind is corrupt, so there is no need to discuss it further. As for science, we only need to look at the cycle of life to see that it is cruel. Because of the fall (Genesis 2), nature has become cruel. Animals eat each other and can be quite mean. The phrase "it's a dog-eat-dog world" is used to describe how rough nature can be. As it comes to psychology, renowned psychologist Jordan Peterson, in his book *12 Rules for Life*, writes that "when once naive people recognize in themselves the seeds of evil and monstrosity, and see themselves as dangerous."[20] He writes this while discussing how some soldiers experience PTSD (post-traumatic stress disorder) because of what they did on the battlefield. They realize that they are capable of evil, and this is a shocking revelation to them. Peterson believes that there is a monster inside all of us, no matter how "good" we think we are.

The Noahic covenant shows that while God loves His world and that it needs to be cared for, it is not pure but evil and corrupt. Biology shows us that nature can be cruel. We see this in the circle of life, natural disasters, disease, and aging. If life were good, we would not have these things. But since there are many unfortunate things that occur outside of mankind's influence, it is clear that life would not be better or worse if we were absent.

---

cessed 9 May 2022.

20 Peterson, Jordan B. *12 Rules for Life: An Antidote to Chaos*. Toronto Random House Canada, 2018, p. 25.

We cannot save this world; it is slowly dying no matter what we do to stop it, nor can nature save us. Only Christ can do that. Again, to focus on anything outside of Christ as savior is heresy and contrary to Scripture. This is the fallacy of Neo-Gnosticism, to focus on this world as the cure (by thinking that turning toward nature or politics can save us from the decay of the world) instead of the true cure: Christ.

The Preciousness of Life

God instituted two new things for mankind after the flood. The first new institution was the giving of animals as food. Before the flood, the sons of God were herbivores. God had not given them meat for food yet. After the flood, God told Noah that meat was now admissible to eat. The only stipulation was that man could not drink the blood.[21]

It is believed that God told Noah that man could now eat meat to show that only life can come from death. This was to show that God requires death for life. This is a small example of the greater reality of salvation. This also was the precursor to religious sacrifice that was required for the Mosaic law. God allowed the killing of animals for food.

The second change was more like a clarification of expectations. This is when God clarifies that life is precious to Him. It is precious because He made it and that it is His to give or take.[22]

This statement has two important ramifications. A Neo-Gnostic's argument against capital punishment is that a God of love would not judge an individual for taking a life.[23] As usual, this is the wrong thing to focus on. The real issue is how could a

---

[21] Genesis 9:3–4

[22] Genesis 9:5–6

[23] Nomad. "Why a Christian Can't Support the Death Penalty." *Nomad,* 31 Mar. 2015, www.patheos.com/blogs/revangelical/2015/03/31/why-a-christian-cant-support-the-death-penalty.html. Accessed 10 May 2022.

loving God allow an individual to destroy a gift that He has given? Life is precious, and He has crafted every individual personally. If someone takes that life from God, then their life is required to replace it.

Mankind was created in the image of God, and God takes that very seriously. In Genesis 1:26,[24] God shows how much we mean to Him. He would not make us out of His image and just allow us to kill each other without any consequences. God even goes as far as saying that if an animal kills a person, God requires it to be killed as payment.[25] If God requires judgment on animals that slay an individual, how much more would He require of an individual who kills a brother or sister.

The second ramification is abortion. If God views life as precious, then He would be against the murder of unborn children. A keyword in the passage is the lifeblood. God does not focus on mental development or technical-scientific terminology. God says if there is lifeblood running in their veins, they should not be killed. Unborn children have blood; therefore, they easily fall into this category. For argument's sake, unborn children develop arteries and veins around day 15–16.[26] This shows that blood is one of the first things developed in a child. There are other reasons God gives against murder and abortion, but these are the reasons given in this covenant.

Lastly, God destroyed the world by flood because He said that all aspects of their thoughts were corrupt.[27] Obviously, this

---

[24] The ESV says, "Then God said, 'Let us make man in our image, after our likeness…'"

[25] Genesis 9:5

[26] "Development of Blood Vessels and Fetal Circulation | Anatomy and Physiology II." *Lumenlearning.com*, 2022, courses.lumenlearning.com/suny-ap2/chapter/development-of-blood-vessels-and-fetal-circulation/#:~:text=Blood%20cells%20and%20vessel%20production,begins%20approximately%202%20days%20later.. Accessed 10 May 2022.

[27] Genesis 6:5

raises one important question. Was their sin more sinful than our sin is today?

No, their sin was not better or worse than our sin is today. Sin to God is sin. Its punishment is death. God states that the heart and mind of man were evil. It was not the environment or social structure that was evil, but the people themselves. As we have discussed before, a system cannot be evil if the people who make up the system are good. A system can be good only if the individuals in it act in a good manner or are encouraged to act well. But this world is corrupt and is full of corrupt individuals. In Genesis 8:21 (ESV),[28] we hear God say that mankind is evil from the beginning. This type of dialogue is not a new conclusion for God based on decisions made by mankind. This is a clarifying statement for the benefit of man so that we understand what God thinks or feels.

Warning and Guidance Before Judgment

One part of the covenant is that He will never destroy the world suddenly. God hinted with Adam that He was going to send a savior, but now He is promising that He will not destroy the world without pre-knowledge of judgment.[29] God will judge the world again, but He is promising that He will give us warning, a savior, and plenty of time to learn love and follow Him. He established the rainbow to remind us of this promise. Every time the heavens break open and rain pours from the sky, we can look up and see the glorious bow stretching across the sky. We can take heart that God is still there. His promises still hold.

---

[28] …the LORD said in his heart, "I will never again curse the ground because of man, for the intention of man's heart is evil from his youth…

[29] Genesis 8:20–22

Abrahamic Covenant

Many years passed between Noah and Abraham. Though, we have no idea how long. We have genealogies that link Noah to Abraham. But this is as detailed as we can get to the time between them and the date that they lived.

During these years, mankind started to spread and repopulate the world as God had desired. By the time Abraham was born,[30] civilization had started in Mesopotamia.[31] Abraham was born in the city of Ur, but he would spend his more important years in Canaan. He is considered the first father of Israel, God's chosen people. God made two promises with him, but we classify them under the same covenant. The first promise was to make Abraham a great nation, and the second promise was that salvation would enter the world through him and his family.

Understanding this covenant is important because many Neo-Gnostics consider Jesus as a moral teacher, not as God. If we can show that God was planning to send Jesus since the beginning of sin, we gain one more way to disprove this claim. As we mentioned above, each covenant moves mankind one more step toward Christ.

First, God promises the land of Canaan to Abraham's children. This is done in Genesis 12:7.[32] God was signaling out Abraham and his descendants to be used as His chosen nation. They were not chosen for their prowess or their wisdom. Nor were they chosen because God needed them. God chose them because He wanted to, and He wanted to show His love and steadfastness through a specific people. God was showing that

---

[30] Believed to be somewhere between 2,300 and 1,900 B.C.

[31] *Timemaps.com*, 2021, www.timemaps.com/civilizations/ancient-mesopotamia/. Accessed 10 May 2022.

[32] Then the LORD appeared to Abram and said, "To your offspring I will give this land." So he built there an altar to the LORD, who had appeared to him.

when He makes a promise, it will come to pass. The first way He showed this was by giving them Isaac as He had promised. Sarah was past her birthing years, yet God blessed her with a child anyway.

God makes covenants with us knowing we will never hold up our side of the bargain[33] but because He is merciful, loving, and consistent. The final reason why He chose a nation was to show the path from Adam to a savior. This is partly why genealogies were important in the Jewish culture.

The contract between God and Abram happens in Genesis 15:7–21.[34] In reality, this contract was between God and Himself, though it concerned Abraham and God. The ceremony mentioned in this passage was a very common practice at that time. The key part of the ceremony is when the signers walk between the animals. When two kings wanted to make covenants between their nations, both parties would walk between the animals. The symbolism was that whoever broke the prom-

---

[33] Which is to follow and worship God

[34] And he said to him, "I am the LORD who brought you out from Ur of the Chaldeans to give you this land to possess." But he said, "O Lord God, how am I to know that I shall possess it?" He said to him, "Bring me a heifer three years old, a female goat three years old, a ram three years old, a turtledove, and a young pigeon." ... Then the LORD said to Abram, "Know for certain that your offspring will be sojourners in a land that is not theirs and will be servants there, and they will be afflicted for four hundred years. But I will bring judgment on the nation that they serve, and afterward they shall come out with great possessions. As for you, you shall go to your fathers in peace; you shall be buried in a good old age. And they shall come back here in the fourth generation, for the iniquity of the Amorites is not yet complete." When the sun had gone down and it was dark, behold, a smoking fire pot and a flaming torch passed between these pieces. On that day the LORD made a covenant with Abram, saying, "To your offspring I give this land, from the river of Egypt to the great river, the river Euphrates, the land of the Kenites, the Kenizzites, the Kadmonites, the Hittites, the Perizzites, the Rephaim, the Amorites, the Canaanites, the Girgashites and the Jebusites."

ise would become like the animals, killed, and split in two. This was a very powerful and symbolic statement.

In this situation, God walks through by Himself. He does this by showing that man does not need to uphold any commands for God to keep up His side. This makes this covenant an unconditional covenant. While we are a part of the covenant, we have no part in upholding it. This is important because we are incapable of upholding any covenant with God. No matter how many times we mess up, which is daily, we cannot lose the promise of this covenant.

Abraham, a sinful man, would break any covenant made with God. But God was the only person who walked between the animals, symbolizing that only He needed to uphold His side of the bargain for the covenant to remain intact. This promise God has kept even though His people did every wrong thing possible.

Necessity of Circumcision

This section also had a subclause: circumcision. There was no way that Abraham could have broken his covenant with God, but God wanted an outward sign of this covenant. Genesis 17:11 (ESV) says, "You shall be circumcised in the flesh of your foreskins, and it shall be a sign of the covenant between me and you." God wanted His people to stand out amongst the rest of the world. He wanted the way they acted and looked to outwardly symbolize the purity they were supposed to have from God.

God wanted His people to look and act differently. Our love for God should drive us to follow His commands, but this was before the law. Abraham did not have to follow the Mosaic law because it did not exist yet. What Abraham had to follow was the moralistic law.[35] As mentioned before, there is a drastic

[35] This is the only law that we have to follow now as well.

difference between the moral law (a general rule of right living)[36] and the civil law. The civil law was only to be followed by the nation of Israel while they were a nation. The moral law is to still be followed because these are the things that surpass the physical requirements of a code of law.

Mosaic Covenant

God's third covenant with mankind was made with Moses on Mount Sinai. This is the second promise to Israel and can be seen as a continuation of the Abrahamic covenant. God promised that He would make them a great nation, which is what He told Abraham. The difference here is that God gave them specific laws and commandments to follow. Up to this point in Scripture, God had given simple commands. Do not eat that, populate the world, worship Me. Things like that. Now He is showing through a code of law that mankind cannot achieve perfection by living a perfect life. Primarily this is because we cannot live perfectly. We cannot even be good for a few hours without messing up. If we cannot do that, how can we be perfect?

God had always expected His people to conduct themselves morally, but He had not specified such commandments as dietary restrictions or land customs. His commandments on Sinai were both to set His people apart and to give them healthy restrictions. This is where we receive the civil and religious laws, but the moral laws were issued at creation when man was still in the garden.

This covenant is found in Exodus 19:4–6[37] and is one of the few covenants that are bilateral. God will always love us and

---

[36] Merriam-Webster Dictionary. "Moral." *Merriam-Webster.com*, 2022, www.merriam-webster.com/dictionary/moral%20law. Accessed 10 May 2022.

[37] 'You yourselves have seen what I did to the Egyptians, and how I bore you

His creation and will always love Israel, but the blessings in this covenant can be taken away. God is a God of love as well as justice. If His people do not follow His commandments, He will remove His blessings from them. A common question that stems from verses like this is: "Why would a loving and merciful God promise something that He would just take away?"

This is a very popular type of question for Neo-Gnostics. As we discussed in chapter six, when we view God's love incorrectly, He would not do anything to harm His people, no matter what. When our ideas on love are incorrect, we cannot fathom why God would do anything that displeases us. Self-focused love makes it hard to understand how disciplining can actually be more loving than letting the person continue their destructive path.

While this is a good question, the issue is the focus. Focusing on one aspect of God and forgetting all other aspects of God is a major issue. God is not just a God of love or a God of wrath. God is complex, and we cannot comprehend Him. He is fully loving and fully holy. This means that when He does something, He expects perfection. If we fail to achieve that standard, He cannot let it slide. If He let people frivolously disobey His commands without consequence, He would not be God, nor would He be loving. Just as a parent does not let their child live in foolishness, our Father does not let us pursue destructive desires without judgment.[38]

There is one more reason why the Mosaic law was made. God did not change the criteria for salvation, but He created the

---

on eagles' wings and brought you to myself. Now therefore, if you will indeed obey my voice and keep my covenant, you shall be my treasured possession among all peoples, for all the earth is mine; and you shall be to me a kingdom of priests and a holy nation.' These are the words that you shall speak to the people of Israel.

[38] We are children. We want our Father to give us candy, but we do not want to deal with the stomachache. We want His stability, but we do not want His rules.

law to show us our inability for self-salvation. The people of Israel were not saved by their works or by following the law. The patriarchs and David knew that they were not saved by the law but by faith. David wrote about his unworthiness and his need for mercy.[39] Also, in Hebrews 11:4–12, the author writes that Abel and Enoch were saved by faith, not by their sacrifices or actions. We do not derive salvation from the law. The law was made to show us our depravity.

The law was created to show that we required a savior. As mentioned above, we are unable to save ourselves. This is a common issue for Neo-Gnostics because they want to get to God by following whatever path they want. By giving us the law, God was showing that no matter how hard we tried, we would always fall short. Those who truly understood God understood that the law was not made to save but to condemn (Romans 3:19–20).[40]

Those who did not understand the mercy of God tried to save themselves by following the law perfectly. The problem is that no matter how hard they tried, nor how well they thought they were following it, no one can perfectly follow the law. The payment for our sins is so high that man can never climb high enough to reach it, that is, without the help of Christ.

A great example of this is the mountain of salvation. Imagine being a hiker climbing a mountain. This hiker is trying to reach the top because they believe that by climbing to the summit, they will gain salvation. They climb and climb, but the top is still far away. Every turn they make, they see another turn. The mountain seems to just continue on and on. But even-

---

[39] Psalm 51

[40] Now we know that whatever the law says it speaks to those who are under the law, so that every mouth may be stopped, and the whole world may be held accountable to God. For by works of the law no human being will be justified in his sight, since through the law comes knowledge of sin. — Romans 3:19–20 (ESV)

tually, after what feels like years of persistence, they finally see a glimpse of the top. The hiker sees the destination. At the top, he sees God. If the hiker can reach God, he will have obtained salvation by his own work. Now that he knows he is getting close, he doubles his efforts.

Eventually, he reaches the summit, and excitement overcomes his exhaustion. Glancing in God's direction, he sees that there is a 100-foot chasm separating him from God. His heart drops. The hiker sees a man sitting next to the chasm holding a cross. Curious, he walks up to him, and once he is close enough, he realizes that it is Jesus Christ. After the shock of this realization fades, he asks Him a question.

"Where were you this whole time? I struggled up that mountain on my own. Why are you up here doing nothing?"

Looking down at the hiker, Christ responds with a smile. "You assume that it was by your strength that you ascended the mountain and reached me."

Suddenly life becomes clear: no matter how much work we put into reaching God, he is unobtainable. We can never reach Him unless He reaches for us first. Once an individual reaches this point in their journey, there is only one conclusion: overwhelming gratitude. Once we reach the summit, through the strength and grace of God, Christ will lay the cross down across the chasm, and we can walk to our heavenly Father. There is no other way to God.

There really is only one option if we have climbed the right mountain. It is by God alone through grace that we make it up His mountain. The mountain of works is unending. The path that ascends its side goes on and on in endless circles. This is the difference between the law and grace. The law leaves us angry and bitter, while grace leaves us free and happy.

Palestinian Covenant

> *If your outcasts are in the uttermost parts of heaven, from there the LORD your God will gather you, and from there he will take you. And the LORD your God will bring you into the land that your fathers possessed, that you may possess it. And he will make you more prosperous and numerous than your fathers. (*
>
> —Deuteronomy 30:4–5 ESV

> *The LORD your God will make you abundantly prosperous in all the work of your hand, in the fruit of your womb and in the fruit of your cattle and in the fruit of your ground. For the LORD will again take delight in prospering you, as he took delight in your fathers…*
>
> —Deuteronomy 30:9 ESV

This covenant is the third installment in the Israeli blessings. God promised Abraham to give them what is now modern-day Palestine, and He promised Moses that He would make Israel a great nation. Unlike the Mosaic covenant, this one is unconditional. God is restating his promise to Abraham in that He will always care for Israel. He will always give them their promised land, and He will always bring their hearts back to Him. God also says that He will bring more prosperity to Abraham's children than He did to Abraham.

Historically, the first part of this promise has been fulfilled twice. After Israel and Judah were conquered and dispersed amongst the Babylonians and the Persian empires, God brought them back to Israel and had them reestablished. Judah was conquered in 586 B.C., and they started their return back to Judah between 538 and 444 B.C. Their return happened in three different sections within a 93-year period.[41]

They stayed in their promised land for about 600 years. During this period, Israel no longer wandered away from God as their ancestors did. Instead, Israel clasped onto the law and created a system of fake purity. This period includes the 400 years of silence and ends with the birth of Jesus.

The second dispersion happened in the year 70 A.D. Rome sieged and sacked Jerusalem.[42] This time, they would remain outcasts spread across the world for almost two millennia. Israel would not become a recognized nation until 1948, after England restored land to the Jews.[43] The Zionist movement encouraged and campaigned for Jews to return to the promised land. Today Israel is a nation and has been persecuted by both its direct neighbors as well as from nations across the globe. It is unknown if God's people will be scattered again. Whether they are or not, one thing is clear: God will always reestablish His people to their land. His promises are always kept.

The second part of the Palestinian covenant can also be seen throughout history. God says that He will make His people prosperous in everything that they do. Even though Jews have been persecuted by almost every group near them, they have always prospered. During the Medieval period, Jews had difficulty finding places to call home. Europe believed that the

---

41 "Babylonian Exile." *Bibleodyssey.org*, 2022, www.bibleodyssey.org/en/places/main-articles/babylonian-exile. Accessed 10 May 2022.

42 "The Diaspora." *Jewishvirtuallibrary.org*, 2022, www.jewishvirtuallibrary.org/the-diaspora. Accessed 10 May 2022.

43 "Milestones: 1945–1952 - Office of the Historian." *State.gov*, 2022, history.state.gov/milestones/1945-1952/creation-isra-el#:~:text=On%20May%2014%2C%201948%2C%20David,nation%20on%20the%20same%20day.. Accessed 10 May 2022.

Jews murdered Jesus, making them evil creatures deserving death.[44] But even with this view, Jews still prospered financially and culturally.

By the twentieth century, Jews in countries like Germany, America, and England had worked their way up into the upper echelons of society. The Jews made up about 1% of the German population around the beginning of the 1930s,[45] but they made up around 30% of the rich and educated.[46] This is proof that God blesses His people no matter what happens. His hand is always with them.

God made these promises to show that He can fulfill them no matter what mankind tries to do. Neo-Gnostics have a hard time believing that God is powerful enough to complete His promises. If God can keep His people alive and prosperous, how much more can He do to save our eternal souls?

Davidic Covenant

One unique aspect of God's covenants is that they bounce between general and personal. First, God made a covenant with Adam; then He made one with the whole earth. The next covenant is with Abraham (personal) and then with Israel (which comes in two sections which are the Mosaic and Palestinian covenants). The last two covenants are with David (personal again) and then with all of mankind (general).

---

[44] "Anti-Judaism before the Enlightenment." *Facing History and Ourselves*, 2022, www.facinghistory.org/holocaust-and-human-behavior/chapter-2/anti-judaism-enlightenment. Accessed 10 May 2022.

[45] "Germany: Jewish Population in 1933." *Ushmm.org*, 2022, encyclopedia.ushmm.org/content/en/article/germany-jewish-population-in-1933. Accessed 10 May 2022.

[46] Metaxas, Eric. *Bonhoeffer: Pastor, Martyr, Prophet, Spy*. Nashville, Thomas Nelson, 2010, p. 110.

This is the last personal covenant made with an individual. Now that God had promised to bring the savior into the world through Abraham's children, He decided to pick a family. King David's line was that line. Just like when He chose Israel to be His chosen nation, He did not choose David because of any specific goodness. God chose David because he wanted to; it's that simple. While David was a great king, God did not choose him based on this fact.

Like the Abrahamic and Palestinian covenants, the Davidic covenant is also a unilateral, unconditional covenant. God did not require anything of David; thus, David could not mess up the covenant. God promised to save the world through David, and there was nothing David could do about it, which is a relief on our part.

Inside the Davidic Covenant

The Davidic covenant can be broken up into three different sections. The first part was the creation of a dynasty based on David's family. The second part is the kingdom of Israel under that dynasty. And lastly, God promised that Christ, a decedent of David, would live the perfect life and save the world.

God promised David that his family would reign over Israel for many generations. This royal dynasty would end when Babylon conquered Judah. David's family no longer ruled Israel or Judah, but his family line would still survive.

One practice of Israel was precise lineage keeping. Every child who was born to a Hebrew family would have their name written down so that familial lines could be concretely kept.[47] This is how we know that Jesus was the descendant of David.

---

47 "The Importance of Messianic Genealogy." *Christian Courier*, 2022, www.christiancourier.com/articles/1556-the-importance-of-messianic-genealogy. Accessed 10 May 2022.

Matthew 1:1–16 lines out the lineage of Joseph from Abraham, while Luke 3:23–38 is believed to be Mary's.[48]

Before Saul and David were crowned, Israel was a theocracy. A theocracy is a form of rule in which a god rules, not an earthly king. For Israel, this meant following the commandments and laws given in the Mosaic covenant. From the time of Moses to the crowning of Saul, Israel was a theocracy. When God needed to save or judge His people, He would send a specific individual. These are the individuals mentioned in the book of Judges. They were pseudo rulers that did not continue their reign through a descendent. When a judge died, their rule ended. Usually, shortly after, Israel would fall back into sin, and the cycle would start over again, showing how much we need an everlasting savior.

When Saul was crowned, Israel became a kingdom like the nations around them, which is what they wanted. Saul did not follow God, nor was He the king that God had chosen. After Saul was killed by the Philistines, David rose to the throne. David had been crowned king before this, but He waited until God's time for Saul's reign to end.[49]

As previously stated, David was God's chosen king. As the chosen ruler of Israel, God promised him that his kingdom would last forever. Even though his dynasty ended with the first fall of Jerusalem in 586 B.C.,[50] God promised that he would reestablish his throne, and it would never end.[51] This second

---

[48] There is some debate on whose genealogy is being followed in Luke's since it ends with Joseph (just like Matthew's) but diverges on two separate points. But this does not take away from the main point, which is that Jesus is of the Davidic line.

[49] I Samuel 24:6

[50] Babylonian Exile." *Bibleodyssey.org*, 2022, www.bibleodyssey.org/en/places/main-articles/babylonian-exile. Accessed 10 May 2022.

[51] II Samuel 7:1–17

promise ties directly into the last part of the covenant, which is Christ.

God promised Adam that He would send a savior to save the world. This savior, called the second Adam, would live the perfect life that Adam was supposed to live and would be able to die for the sins of the world. Jesus was the fulfillment of the promise made to both Adam and David. Jesus was fully God and fully man and was born of the line of David. He came to the earth to fulfill the promise to Adam and then ascended into heaven and sits on a throne, fulfilling the promise to David. Jesus is our savior and defendant. He sits on the right hand of God, reigning as king and priest.

New Covenant

The entire Old Testament and all of the covenants lead to this one new covenant. That is because this covenant is the fulfillment of Christ and His mission. Everything disciples of Christ believe rests on Christ and His works.

Salvation has always been based on the works that Christ was going to do. We now live in a period where sacrifice is not needed because the eternal sacrifice has already been completed. But in the age before Christ, sacrifices were still required. These sacrifices did not save, but they pointed to Christ, the eternal lamb.[52]

The new covenant ended sacrifices. We no longer have to sacrifice to remove the blemish of sin. Christ has now come, and we now live under the promise that Christ will intercede for us forever (Hebrews 9:13–15).[53] God no longer sees our sin

---

[52] "And by that will we have been sanctified through the offering of the body of Jesus Christ once for all." —Hebrews 10:10 (ESV)

[53] "For if the blood of goats and bulls, and the sprinkling of defiled persons with the ashes of a heifer, sanctify for the purification of the flesh, how much more will the blood of Christ, who through the eternal Spirit offered

because Christ stands between us and His Father and intercedes for us. This is what makes the new covenant so impactful and different than the rest. God sent His son, who is part of the trinity, to purify us and act as our lawyer. This is not done in any other religion. Our God came down and did the work for us. Other gods just watch their believers struggle and laugh, or in some cases, they try to kill them. God saw the struggle and knew that we needed someone to intercede for us. So, He came down and did the work. He lowered Himself to the lowliest position possible and died the most horrendous death. This covenant was sealed in the blood of God, and it cannot ever be undone or washed away.

All Lead to This One Promise

This is the last and most encompassing covenant between God and His creation. This covenant incorporates Jews and gentiles. No other promise made by God includes individuals outside of His chosen people.[54] This promise is the one that all mankind has been longing for. No other religion has a God that was willing to come down and endure the humiliation, pain, and loneliness that Jesus endured for us. All of the other covenants led to this one promise. God promised Abraham a promised land and that his name would be made great. He promised David that his family would rule forever, and He promised Adam that He would redeem mankind from the sin that he caused to enter the world. All of these promises were fulfilled in Christ.

---

himself without blemish to God, purify our conscience from dead works to serve the living God. Therefore he is the mediator of a new covenant, so that those who are called may receive the promised eternal inheritance, since a death has occurred that redeems them from the transgressions committed under the first covenant." —Hebrews 9:13–15 (ESV)

[54] Except for the Noahic covenant since Israel did not exist

Ending Remarks

Many Neo-Gnostics believe that God loves us dearly but does not have much of a plan. They believe that God is allowing us to write the story of this world without any true intervention. They believe that it is knowledge that saves, not really Christ. The covenants mentioned in this chapter show otherwise.

Each covenant reveals the true heart of God and how much He cares for us. Each covenant becomes more and more personal and intimate. The Adamic covenant is vague and impersonal, but by the time that the new covenant is established, God has become man.[55] He has died for our sins and has given us the Holy Spirit[56] to dwell in our newly uncalcified hearts.

We must understand what God has done for us. As stated in the opening section, if we do not understand the gift and uniqueness of our faith, our faith falls into the crowd and loses its power. A common debate about Christianity is that our faith is no different than any other religion. This is not true in the slightest. No other religion has a God who was willing to come down to earth, live a humble life in a nondescript family, and die a horrible death.

These covenants are the promises that God made with us that show His love, mercy, and faithfulness. Pagan gods (like the Babylonian and Greek gods) treated their creations like toys who do their whims and play their games. Our God desires a true relationship with His creation, and He has shown that time and time again. Covenants make Christianity unique. They show that we are desired, sought after, and loved.

God has been writing a detailed story pointing to Christ and has allowed us to play important roles within. We could have just as easily been left on the sidelines, but God desired to

---

[55] In Christ

[56] Also God

incorporate us into His plot. Neo-Gnostics claim that they can have a special relationship with God outside of His word. Based on these special covenants, their claims are false. God has made promises to individuals, and they have had special relationships with God. But there is a big difference between the relationships in Scripture and those claimed today. Adam's, Moses's, Abraham's, and David's relationships with God were purposeful. They pointed to Christ and set up examples of how God's plans would occur.

The way that Neo-Gnostics claim their special relationships work just shows how selfish they are. These "revelations" just allow them to follow the path they were already on. God has revealed things to specific people, and there is some argument about whether or not He is still speaking to us as He did in biblical times. If He is, He only does it for gospel purposes. He has never nor will ever reveal something to a person that contradicts what He has already said or done. Not every word of Jesus was written in the gospels. This means that it is possible for Christ to reveal Himself to a person. But, if God reveals Himself to a person and contradicts Scripture, that person has not met God. As we have seen, God reveals Himself only to further His kingdom, not ours.

The covenants show God's detailed interaction with His creation. Believing that God is standoffish is wrong and dangerous. God has spent[57] a lot of energy orchestrating His plan of love and redemption. It has taken thousands of years and hundreds of generations. But we are now standing in the light that Christ has given us. We can share that light with others only because we know what He did and why He did it. We cannot possibly share the good news if we do not understand the effort God went through to breach the void separating His perfect creation from Himself. We may not be perfect now, but one day

---

[57] In human terms

we will be again. That is His desire, and that is what will happen.

9

History

Those who cannot remember the past are condemned to repeat it.[1]

—George Santayana

As we walk farther into the cave we entered previously, we find ourselves in a second corridor. While the last corridor focused on covenants, it seems like this one focuses on the history of the church. There are scenes of the early church and their struggle for truth and against Roman persecution. Later on, there are scenes depicting the Reformation and the Inquisition.

---

1 René Magritte. ""Those Who Cannot Remember the Past Are Condemned to Repeat It."George Santayana, the Life of Reason, 1905. From the Series Great Ideas of Western Man." *Smithsonian American Art Museum*, 2022, americanart.si.edu/artwork/those-who-cannot-remember-past-are-condemned-repeat-it-george-santayana-life-reason-1905#:~:text=America%2C%201984.124.194-,%E2%80%9CThose%20who%20cannot%20remember%20the%20past%20are%20condemned%20to%20repeat,Great%20Ideas%20of%20Western%20Man.. Accessed 10 May 2022.

History is very important, but it is an odd subject. The issue with history is that it requires a mastery of so many different disciplines. To understand church history, the student has to understand politics, theology, and psychology. Politics is studied to understand why kings did and thought what they did and thought. Theology is required[2] because religion is a central piece in most societies, and it needs to be understood to even try and understand the culture. Psychology is always a good study when trying to understand people. The idea that history is a multidisciplinary subject is one of the first things taught to historians in college. With all of these side subjects, history becomes a truly daunting subject to master.

For our purposes, we will only focus on the historical and theological aspects of Christianity. We will also only focus on the church from Christ until now. To study any further back, we would be studying Jewish history, which is definitely a worthy study but not the point of this book. The purpose of this study is to counter the false understandings that Neo-Gnostics have about history, primarily when it comes to how the church canonized Scripture, how women were treated, and how accurate Scripture is.

To begin, we will look at what the early church was like, how they were treated, and how they treated others. Then we will discuss the early process of scriptural canonization. Lastly, we will discuss the translations of Scripture that we have today and how we can trust them.

Secular Sources of the Early Church

When it comes to beginnings, it is sometimes hard to pinpoint a clear one. Some cultures or organizations are so old that their beginnings are covered in mysticism and legends. Still others

[2] At least when it comes to church history

have such stark beginnings that they are like a stamp on the timeline of history. The beginning of Christianity is like the second form of beginnings. Christ's impact on the world was so strong that there were religious and secular historians who have written about His existence. This is important because some individuals in the Neo-Gnostic community believe that Christ did not exist.[3] These secular writings are also important because even more individuals in this community believe that Christianity was an easy religion and that rich, powerful people just converted for the power. This is very wrong historically.

The first and most well-known historian is Tacitus,[4] who wrote an account of Emperor Nero in which he mentions both the persecution of Christians and the crucifixion of Jesus.[5,6] Based on his writings, we can see that a stark opponent of the Jews and Christ acknowledged that He lived and died by crucifixion.[7] We also see that Christians were hated and called abominations. This does not sound like a group of people who lived easy lives full of prosperity and privilege.

---

[3] Tarico, Valerie. "5 Reasons to Suspect That Jesus Never Existed." *Salon*, Salon.com, Sept. 2014, www.salon.com/2014/09/01/5_reasons_to_suspect_that_jesus_never_existed/. Accessed 10 May 2022.

[4] 55–117 A.D.

[5] "Consequently, to get rid of the report, Nero fastened the guilt and inflicted the most exquisite tortures on a class hated for their abominations, called Christians by the populace. Christus, from whom the name had its origin, suffered the extreme penalty during the reign of Tiberius at the hands of on of our procurators, Pontius Pilatus, and a most mischievous superstition, thus checked for the moment, again broke out not only in Judea, the first source of the evil, but even in Rome, where all things hideous and shameful from every part of the word find their center and become popular."

[6] "Tacitus, Suetonius, and the Historical Jesus." *Biblical Christianity*, 20 Feb. 2017, bib.irr.org/tacitus-suetonius-and-historical-jesus.

[7] Extreme penalty is a reference to His way of death.

Nero ruled between 54 A.D. and 68 A.D. and is known for being one of the harshest emperors on Christians.[8] This was also when Christianity was at its weakest. Christianity during this early period was hated, Christians were mutilated, and Jesus was considered a lowly criminal. Not positive things in any situation.

But is Tacitus (who was a historian and public figure in Rome) the only source we have discussing early Christians? No. We also have passages by Phlegon (Greek author of the second century) and Thallus (Greek historian) that mention the eclipse that occurred when Christ was crucified.[9] While they do not mention Christ or His followers directly, their writings back up other facts that are important to Christ's narrative.

Writings by these men prove two things. Firstly, Christ did live. He was an actual historical individual. Romans[10] were all about law and order. They did not live in the mythical worlds like the Greeks or the Norse. While the average person was as spiritual as their counterparts, writers did not write to appease them. They wrote to remember the world as it was. They were known for writings, histories, and political accounts. This makes their mention of Christ more trustworthy.

Their writings also show that darkness did occur when Christ died, and that was not a Jewish mystical moment. It is common when miraculous moments happen for critics to just dismiss them as hocus pocus. But when a secular writer describes the same thing, it is hard to discredit them.

Lastly, these writers show that Christians were real and that the struggles they faced were not faked. Another aspect of

---

[8] "Nero Persecutes the Christians, 64 A.D." *Eyewitnesstohistory.com*, 2022, www.eyewitnesstohistory.com/christians.htm. Accessed 10 May 2022.

[9] Unfortunately, we have lost the actual documents, but their writings are mentioned by Julius Africanus.

[10] The term "Roman" is used in a more general sense in this book. It is being used to mean anyone who lived in the Roman empire.

Christianity that people try to discredit is their persecution and how they were actually welcomed by the paganistic Romans because their beliefs were not that different.

Pliny the Younger (author, lawyer, and magistrate of Rome) wrote about early Christian meeting habits.[11] The way he wrote shows that he was not a Christian but that he was not their biggest enemy either. These sources show that Christians were not fully accepted by society and that they were not always treated the best.

Christian habits were also disliked. They believed in one God, which created some tension between them and the pagans around them. Christians were deemed antisocial because they no longer participated in community feasts or other community gatherings, like going to the theater or the colosseum. This was because sacrifices or immoral acts were done there, and Christians no longer could or wanted to attend.[12] In all, Christians acted differently and believed differently, and this made them outcasts in society. Romans definitely did not want to associate with them when the Roman guards were hunting them down for exile or execution.

The sources we have just seen are only some of the many sources out there on this subject. These are the more popular ones among historians and authors, which is why they were chosen for this work as well. This marks one category that many Neo-Gnostics get hung up on. Now to the next.

---

[11] "They were in the habit of meeting on a certain fixed day before it was light, when they sand in alternate verses a hymn to Christ, as to god, and bound themselves by a solemn oath not to any wicked deeds, not to commit any fraud, theft or adultery, never to falsify their word, nor to deny any trust when they should be call to deliver it up, after which it was their custom to separate, and then reassemble to partake of food "but food of an ordinary but and innocent kind."

[12] Hirt, Herb. "Early Christians in a Pagan World – Israel My Glory." *Israel My Glory*, Feb. 1999, israelmyglory.org/article/early-christians-in-a-pagan-world/.

For White Men Only!

If Christianity was not a popular religion, who would want to follow it? We have already looked at how it was not the religion of the powerful and rich,[13] so does that mean that it was the faith of the poor? Yes … and no. While Christianity did have members from many different social classes, there were very few, if any, from the small wealthy individuals. We are told of rich aristocratic women joining the church in the book of Acts.[14] But it is believed that they were few and were drastically outnumbered by their poorer brethren.

At that time, there really were only two classes: the rich and everyone else. The concept of a middle class did not exist at that time. Most people lived hand to mouth, very few individuals were educated, and life was dangerous no matter what class you lived in. It is crazy to think that the poor in the Western world today live richer lives than the rich in ancient times.[15] This means that the majority of Christians lived in this poor class.

This leads us to why the poorer groups were attracted to Christ while the wealthy disdained Him. What made Christianity attractive was how followers of Christ lived. Even though they were persecuted, they did a number of odd things that made people want to join them. First, they considered themselves aliens of this world. Secondly, they gave heavily to the poor and needy. Lastly, women, children, and slaves were treated better or even as equals in Christian communities.[16]

---

[13] At least not for the early Christians

[14] Acts 9:36 and 16:5–10, to name a couple

[15] We eat better, live longer, and have more comforts than people even one hundred years ago. Our current level of wealth is so much higher than that of our ancestors, it is very hard to imagine what life was like.

[16] "Early Christians and the Care of the Poor | Reflections." *Yale.edu*, 2022, reflections.yale.edu/article/no-more-excuses-confronting-poverty/early-

Since Christians believed that they were not part of this world, they did not act greedily. Believers were more charitable and less likely to take advantage of others. As we discussed previously, Christians are supposed to act with love by serving one another. Hermas (a second-century theologian who wrote *Shepherd of Hermas*) wrote, "assist widows, visit orphans and the poor, ransom God's servants, show hospitality, help oppressed debtors in their need."[17] This was written to explain to the rich how to get into heaven. This abandonment of worldly materialism attracted many pagans.

As we just mentioned, most Romans were poor, or at least on the poorer side of life. Therefore, having an entire group willing to help or even energetic to do so was very unusual. As we saw in the parable of the Good Samaritan, most leaders[18] were too busy to help the average person.[19] We see an example of this in Acts 2[20] when the new believers are willingly selling excess so that they can give to the poor. Christian charity became so well known that even Emperor Julian "the Apostate"[21] once complained, "For it is disgraceful when no Jew is a beggar and the impious Galileans [the name given by Julian to Christians] support our poor in addition to their own."[22]

---

christians-and-care-poor. Accessed 10 May 2022.

17 Inoue, Takanori. "The Early Church's Approach to the Poor in Society and Its Significance to the Church's Social Engagement Today." place.asburyseminary.edu/cgi/viewcontent.cgi?article=1074&context=firstfruitspapers.

18 Whether religious or secular

19 Not a lot has changed when it comes to politicians, it seems.

20 "And they were selling their possessions and belongings and distributing the proceeds to all, as any had need. And day by day, attending the temple together and breaking bread in their homes, they received their food with glad and generous hearts…" —Acts 2:45–46 (ESV)

21 He ruled around 360 A.D.

22 Julian. "Julian: Letter to Arsacius." *www.thenagain.info*,

This type of behavior gave them a good report among the common people. Meaning that Christians looked after the poor and needy whether they were believers or not. This did make a weird imbalanced attitude toward Christians. On the one hand, they were admired for their selflessness and charity. On the other hand, they were mistreated and mistrusted because of those same qualities. This just shows how fickle mankind can be.

Another act that made Christians stand out was their ability, or even willingness, to suffer. Christians were even known to withstand suffering better than the pagans. There were two major epidemics that happened in 165–180 and again in 251–266 that we can look at to see the differences between the pagan outlook and the Christian outlook.

Pagans did not deal with things like plagues well. They believed that it was a punishment from the gods or that, in general, life was pointless. Christians, on the other hand, believed in a purpose in all things. They saw the plagues as a testing of their faith. Because of this, they had a much more positive view even while they were dying. During the second plague, a man by the name of Dionysius wrote that many in his church were sacrificially loving their community by going to the sick and helping them. They were doing this even though they knew that their chances of getting the disease were increasing.[23,24]

---

www.thenagain.info/Classes/Sources/Julian.html.

[23] Most of our brother Christians showed unbounded love and loyalty, never sparing themselves and thinking only of one another. Heedless of danger, they took charge of the sick, attending to their every need and ministering to them in Christ, and with them departed this life serenely happy .... Many, in nursing and curing others, transferred their death to themselves and died in their stead .... The best of our brothers lost their lives in this manner; a number of presbyters, deacons, and laymen winning high commendation so that death in this form, the result of great piety and strong faith, seems in every way the equal of martyrdom.

[24] Inoue, Takanori. "The Early Church's Approach to the Poor in Society and

But so far, we have not really reached the point of this section, have we? We have seen that early Christianity was not a religion of the rich and powerful but for the poor, oppressed, and enslaved. But was it a religion for men? It is now time to look at that question.

To answer the question quickly: no, it was not. Christianity has always welcomed anyone with wide arms,[25] especially when it comes to women. There are many references to important women in Scripture. Some were deacons,[26] others were missionaries, and still others were teachers. Paul mentions many important women who were being used by God for His work: Priscilla,[27] Phoebe,[28] and Junia,[29] to name a few.

It is believed that women consisted of two-thirds of the Christian population. This is very strange since women only consisted of one-third of the populace. We know that early Christianity was full of women by how secular writers wrote. Celsus[30] was very unflattering in his description of Christian conversion.[31] He wrote that only the foolish, dishonorable, the stupid, slaves, and women became Christians.[32] He used these

Its Significance to the Church's Social Engagement Today."

[25] This does not mean that the church has always done a good job showing the love that Christ has for all. Christ came with forgiveness first. He expected change, but He showed love and mercy first. The imperfect church has always had a hard time with this.

[26] In this context, *deacon* is referencing a servant, not a leader of the church.

[27] Acts 18:26 and Romans 16:3–5, among others

[28] Romans 16:1–2

[29] Romans 16:7

[30] Second-century philosopher who disliked Christians

[31] "[Christians] show that they want and are able to convince only the foolish, dishonorable and stupid, only slaves, women and little children"

[32] Kruger, Miachael. "How Early Christianity Was Mocked for Welcoming Women." *Canon Fodder*, 13 July 2020, www.michaeljkruger.com/how-early-

insults because these groups were considered weak and insignificant. Roman society valued war, power, and logic, meaning that slaves, fools, and women were not deemed very high. It was believed that a God who would come down to live a poor life and die could only be worshiped by the weak.[33]

These are just some examples showing that women were just as involved, if not more, than men in early Christianity. This is still true in most churches. Women lead, teach, serve, disciple, and spread the gospel. Some churches regulate women to the sidelines, but this is not the desire of God. There is one last area about women to be touched on, and that is female pastors. This topic is not going to be discussed much in this book because it is a very complicated discussion. To fully unpack this issue, an entire book would be needed. Therefore, let this suffice: women can teach, serve, and disciple. The specific role of pastor is a very narrow title that too many people focus on. It is one small role in the body of Christ. We should not let this one job cause so much strife in the church.

But back to the discussion at hand. Women were treated better by Christians than by pagans. Paul even says that women and men were equals.[34] We have to use the phrase "treated better" because mankind is not, nor will we ever be, perfect. Sadly, we will never treat each other the way God wants us to. But the drastic difference between how Christians treated others and how the secular world did is a great example of the love of God.

---

christianity-was-mocked-for-welcoming-women/.

[33] Kruger, Miachael. "How Early Christianity Was Mocked for Welcoming Women." *Canon Fodder*, 13 July 2020, www.michaeljkruger.com/how-early-christianity-was-mocked-for-welcoming-women/.

[34] 1 Cor. 7:3–5, 1 Cor. 11:11–12, and Gal. 3:26–28

Race and the Early Church

Now that we have looked at how women were treated in the church, there is one last item to look at before we move on. This is: was the church for whites only? This is honestly a terrible question. It shows the ignorance of the asker more than anything else. Though, to be fair, there are many who honestly believe that Christianity was started and perpetuated by white individuals.

First, where does the term *white* come from in relation to race? As we can see, white has been used to describe a color for a long time, but when was it adopted to describe individuals from an entire continent? The first time it was written was in 1613 by playwright Thomas Middleton.[35] The scene in which this word is used is when an African king is describing the faces of some European guests. It is not an insult, just a physical description.

If the term *white* has only been around for about 400 years, it seems to be more of a construction to describe individuals from a generic place. When someone does not know where a person is from,[36] it is easier to describe their physical features. We must remember that the twenty-first-century American outlook on life is a very new one. Not only is it new, but we are such a combination of ethnic groups that it is hard to identify what is what. This is a major strength as well as a weakness. It is amazing how well so many different groups melded together to make entirely new ones. The term European mutt is really the only way to describe most American ancestry, and this is a unique and amazing thing in this country.

---

[35] Simon, Ed. "The Reality of Race: The Term 'White People' Was Invented by a Playwright in 1613." *Scroll.in,* scroll.in/article/850404/the-reality-of-race-the-term-white-people-was-invented-by-a-playwright-in-1613. Accessed 9 Feb. 2022.

[36] As in country, county, or town

But there is one problem, and that is when people do not want to join the cultural melting process. For iron to become steel, it has to be heated hotter than ever and melt away all of the impurities. In a less harsh way, this is what people in America have done. But when individuals want to cling to their way of life and isolate themselves from the rest of the group, they cause issues for both groups. This is the downside of diversity. Both groups start to dislike the other, and that causes a lot of problems. But back to the question at hand.

Since the idea of being *white* did not exist before the seventeenth century, it is hard to believe that anyone would have thought along those lines. To make this concept even more absurd, Christ was a first-century Jew. He lived in Israel, spoke Hebrew,[37] followed Jewish customs, and could trace His lineage to King David and Abraham. He was about as Jewish as was possible. He would have been dark-skinned, dark-haired,[38] and dark-eyed.[39] Not one aspect about Him would have been European.[40]

To add to that, all of His disciples were Jewish. The disciples also went to the Jews first after Christ ascended. Christianity started in Jerusalem and only went from there after some of the disciples were kicked out. It was also a common practice at first to spread the gospel amongst the Jewish communities in

---

[37] And possibly Greek since it was the universal language

[38] With curly hair, unlike a lot of Europeans

[39] Carlton, Genevieve. "What Did Jesus Look Like? Here's What the Evidence Says." *All That's Interesting*, All That's Interesting, 9 Mar. 2022, allthatsinteresting.com/what-did-jesus-look-like. Accessed 13 May 2022.

[40] Though to be fair, the concept of European is also a bad term. Europe spans from the icy north full of light-skinned Vikings to the warm south consisting of darker-skinned Italians. This is what makes this concept even harder to understand. No continent has one type of ethnic group. They are all full of a multitude of people who look, speak, and act differently.

whatever city missionaries went to. Only after they had accepted or rejected the gospel did Gentiles hear of it.

The Bible is full of Jewish and Middle Eastern/African characters practicing Middle Eastern/African customs. There are so few European people mentioned, they could probably be counted on one to two hands. This is what makes the idea that Christianity is a white person's religion ludicrous. Outside of those who honestly do not know better, this is a concept perpetuated by individuals who cannot stand the morals and teachings of Scripture. Christianity is many things, but it is not a religion for or of *white* people.

The Bible

Now that we have discussed how the early church treated people, it is time to look at how the Bible was created. There is a theory that a group of men sat down and edited the Bible to make it read how they wanted it to. This is a popular view by Neo-Gnostics as well as atheists.[41] The problem with this view is that it has no historical backing at all.

The first argument is that there are not a lot of full copies from the original writers. This argument hangs on the idea that as writers copied and translated Scripture, they played a very large game of telephone. Each writer made minute changes that would eventually make the current document untrustworthy. But there is a major issue with this idea.

That issue is that we have thousands of full or partial manuscripts from the ninth century B.C. and onward that prove that the Bible had practically zero alterations. We have more copies of the New Testament than we do of the Old Testament for ob-

---

[41] Phoenix Seminary. "The Council of Nicaea and Biblical Canon - Phoenix Seminary." *Phoenix Seminary*, 25 Apr. 2018, ps.edu/council-nicaea-biblical-canon/. Accessed 13 May 2022.

vious reasons. But the manuscripts[42] that we do have[43] show very little change between copies. There is so little change that the attention to detail is astounding. There are even small grammatical errors that Moses made that were passed on when copied because the writers did not want to change any part of the Torah.[44] This amount of reverence for the text is amazing.

When it comes to the New Testament, things become a little clearer. Since this part of Scripture was written when writing had progressed and society was more stable, there are a lot more manuscripts to look at. There are 10,000 Latin manuscripts, 5,800 Greek manuscripts, and 9,300 manuscripts in other languages.[45] This totals to 25,100 ancient manuscripts. Again, there has been very little change between copies, showing that the Bible we hold today is the same now as it was 1,900 years ago.

We can contrast this number by looking at other popular ancient works like *The Iliad, The Gallic Wars,* and *The Histories of Herodotus. The Iliad* is a very popular work by Homer describing

---

[42] Bell, Sheri. "Ancient Manuscripts That Validate the Bible's Old Testament." *Josh.org,* 14 Feb. 2018, www.josh.org/manuscript-validate-old-testament/?mwm_id=241874010218&mot=J79GNF&gclid=Cj0KCQiAoNWOBhCwARIsAAiHnEh0HgPrPEkX-hwYRzSWvKE-YxOEfgC1VmBRtCAghM0sl9_rKZ0r9uFEaAjZ8EALw_wcB. Accessed 6 Jan. 2022.

[43] The Masoretic Text, The Dead Sea Scrolls, The Samaritan Pentateuch, The Nash Papyrus, and The Silver Amulets

[44] Speak, Moses. "Does Moses Speak Broken Hebrew?" *Biblical Hermeneutics Stack Exchange,* 4 Apr. 2012, hermeneutics.stackexchange.com/questions/1441/does-moses-speak-broken-hebrew. Accessed 13 May 2022.

[45] "Biblical Manuscript." *Wikipedia,* 20 Apr. 2020, simple.wikipedia.org/wiki/Biblical_manuscript#:~:text=There%20are%20over%205%2C800%20complete. Accessed 6 Jan. 2022.

the fabled war of Troy. *The Gallic Wars* was written by Caesar and discusses the Gallic wars. Herodotus was a Greek historian who wrote about his travels and the wars raging around the Mediterranean. *The Iliad* and Herodotus' histories would have been written near the same period as the Old Testament, while Caesar's *The Gallic Wars* would have been right before the New Testament. The only one of these ancient manuscripts to have over 1,000 known copies is *The Iliad*. And it only has around 1,900.[46,47] It is interesting that we have so many manuscripts of the Bible, and yet people still question its validity while they never question works like Herodotus' histories.

Issues Solved by Scripture

Having this many manuscripts solves one of two problems for Scripture. It solves the manuscripts' authenticity issue. This issue, as stated above, is that the book we have now is not the same as the ones written thousands of years ago. We can see that we do not have a forgery or a mistranslated copy. We have the original words to work off of when making modern translations.

The second issue that manuscript support cannot solve is historical accuracy. We may have 25,100 copies of Scripture, but if the information is wrong, it would not matter. A wrong fact written 25,000 times does not suddenly make that fact correct.[48] This is why we have to rely on secular histories and archeologi-

---

46 McDowell, Josh. "Testing the Historical Reliability of the Old Testament." *Jesus Film Project*, www.jesusfilm.org/blog-and-stories/testing-historical-reliability-old-testament.html. Accessed 6 Jan. 2022.

47 "Homer before Print - Homer in Print - the University of Chicago Library." *Www.lib.uchicago.edu*, www.lib.uchicago.edu/collex/exhibits/homer-print-transmission-and-reception-homers-works/homer-print/.

48 This is the same issue that evolution falls into. Adding more years does not suddenly make spontaneous mutation possible.

cal findings to prove parts of Scripture. As we have discussed before, when history proves Scripture correct, we can look at things like the number of manuscripts as extra proof that the Bible is right. It takes both to prove the earthly parts of Scripture. The following paragraphs will discuss that Scripture is what the disciples of Christ claim it to be.

Canonization

When it comes to canonization,[49] there are two main questions we need to ask. The first question is how was the book we have in Scripture deemed inspired by God, and the second question is did people remove books that should have been included? These are important questions because the rest of our answers rest on the accuracy of God's word. If we have incorrect books, then our understanding of God is wrong or incomplete. That can cause some major issues.

Our investigation will be divided into two sections: Old Testament canon and New Testament canon. This is because the two sections were created in entirely different ways. The Old Testament traces the history of Israel and its interactions with God and the prophets. The New Testament is divided between the gospels, which are different tellings of Jesus's life, and letters written by the apostles.

But, to quickly answer the first question: yes, there were strict rules that a book had to follow before it could be considered inspired by God. This primarily comes by looking at the strict requirements that the Jews and then the church applied to writings claiming to be inspired by God. Also, to answer the second question: no, people did not remove or add books that should not have been there.

---

[49] Any official collection of works by an author or a religion

Old Testament Canon

The Old Testament is argued over less than the New Testament when it comes to this topic. Since the Old Testament was written much slower and by more authors, it was able to be tested and generally agreed upon. By the time Jesus walked the earth, the entire Old Testament had been cemented. The only real differences are punctuation and book order. The order of words in English versions might change between editions, but this does not change the reliability of the translations. Also, the order of books in the Bible has differed throughout the centuries, but this also does not change reliability. While these can change the emphasis quite a bit, there really is not much of a difference.

The only other difference is that some groups add some books like the book of Maccabees while others do not. This does show that there are still some arguments over which books can be added to Scripture and which cannot. Some books are added alongside Scripture, meaning that they are not God-inspired but still good books to read.

The real argument comes when discussing the New Testament. This is when things start to get heated. There are many books[50] that are not included in the New Testament that many believe should be. So how do we differentiate between these books that some believe should be included with those that are included?

There are three different criteria that a book must fulfill to be considered canon worthy. First, there is apostolic origin which means that a book was either written by an apostle or by someone directly under an apostle. Second is recognition by the church, which means that the early church recognized the book as having apostolic origin. Lastly is apostolic content, which means that the teachings in the book matched the verbal teach-

---

[50] Usually called the Gnostic Gospels

ings of the apostles. Let us now look at these and see what exactly they mean.

Apostolic origin means one of two things. It means that a book either had to have been written by an apostle specifically, or it had to have been written under the supervision of an apostle. An apostle was one of the specified men chosen by God for this specific task. They included the twelve disciples plus Paul and Matthias. These are the only apostles of the church. So, books written by them or under their supervision would fulfill this first requirement. No other author could claim apostolic origin, though many have tried.

The next criterium is how did the early church accept the book? This focuses on many of the epistles[51] sent to many of the early churches. Most, if not all, of the epistles were written by or under an apostle. Therefore, if the church accepted it as coming from one of the fourteen mentioned above, it would have been considered having the authority of God. Thus, we should also consider it God-inspired.

The last criterium deals with doctrine. A book had to agree with the teachings taught by the apostles during their lifetimes. This means that if a book was written after their death, it could still have been written by someone else who had worked closely with an apostle. But, if the teachings in the book diverted from the known teachings, then it was a forgery.[52]

A great example is the book of Thomas. This book was said to have been written by or under the apostle Thomas. But the teachings in the book do not follow the teachings of the apostles

---

[51] Letters

[52] "What Criteria Were Used to Determine the Canon of Scripture?" *BiblicalTraining.org*, 2012, www.biblicaltraining.org/blog/curious-christian/7-10-2012/what-criteria-were-used-determine-canon-scripture. Accessed 13 May 2022.

when they lived. Thus, it was not canonized. It was later found to be a Gnostic forgery.[53]

This may seem like a simple way of canonization, but it is far from it. These three criteria are very strict and took many years to fully flush out all of the books we have today. By the time of Constantine, the Bible was set.[54] This dispels one major fallacy of modern Neo-Gnostics. They claim that Constantine forced the church to add or remove books that he liked or disliked. This is not true. The council of Nicaea[55] met to discuss Arianism, the nature of Christ, and many other important religious matters of their day. It had nothing to do with Biblical canonization, as many Neo-Gnostics claim.[56]

Ending Remarks

This shows that Scripture was created much slower and by a lot more people than just one old white man. Scripture was made by God, and we used His specific criteria to lay it out. He appointed specific individuals to write down what He wanted. They wrote it, and He spoke it. This is why there is such a strong push for Scripture alone. Every time that mankind tries to add to what God has decreed, things go bad. This is what the rabbis tried to do during the time of Jesus.

---

53 Guest. "Why the Gospel of Thomas Isn't in the Bible." *Cross Examined*, 7 Sept. 2019, crossexamined.org/why-the-gospel-of-thomas-isnt-in-the-bible/. Accessed 13 May 2022.

54 History.com Editors. "The Bible." *HISTORY*, HISTORY, 19 Jan. 2018, www.history.com/topics/religion/bible#:~:text=The%20Muratorian%20Canon%2C%20which%20is,basic%20agreement%20on%20Biblical%20canon.. Accessed 13 May 2022.

55 One of the first church councils, which met in 325

56 "First Council of Nicaea | Description, History, Significance, & Facts | Britannica." *Encyclopædia Britannica*, 2022, www.britannica.com/event/First-Council-of-Nicaea-325. Accessed 13 May 2022.

Instead of just taking the commands of God as they were, Jewish rabbis created a very complicated and arduous set of rules to help Israel stay pure for God. Their intentions were mostly good, but their actions were corrupt. Eventually, they relied more on their set of rules than they did on God. The same can be said with the Catholic church. They have so many traditions and added rules not found in Scripture that they can get caught up in their own religious actions than staying close to God.

This is why staying close to Scripture is so important. God speaks through it every day. There are other ways to converse with God,[57] but Scripture is an easy way to be with Him. This is why we have to know if we can trust the Bible we have before us. If it has been mistranslated, then we are in trouble. This is why the discussion that Neo-Gnostics are having is not a bad one. The issue is that they are approaching it incorrectly.

As we discussed in previous chapters, they are approaching scriptural authenticity based on our culture, not based on Scripture itself. They want certain things to be correct; therefore, they rework or remove whatever they do not like. When Scripture speaks on how men and women are to behave, Neo-Gnostics get angry. When Scripture speaks on marriage being between a man and a woman, they claim homophobia. When Scripture says that all are evil and need a savior, they throw the book down and walk away.

We cannot approach God with our own list of dos and don'ts. Culture grows and fades. It changes with the seasons just like a tree. Sometimes a culture is healthy, and sometimes it is sick. Either way, it is not perfect. We cannot investigate Scripture based on a changing concept. If a person does not like what Scripture has to say, that is totally fine. But if Scripture is correct, they will spend the rest of eternity with God's back facing them. They did not want Him in this life; therefore, He will let

[57] Prayer is an obvious example.

them experience that for eternity. We have to approach the authenticity of Scripture humbly. We must look at the evidence for and against it and weigh what we find.

Does the evidence show that Scripture is authentic and that it has not been corrupted over the years? Or are we working with a book that has been manipulated by countless individuals over centuries? These are not small questions that we ask ourselves. The answer can either shatter the Western world or heal the growing rift. But, we must ask the hard questions. As we discussed in chapter one, we have to deconstruct our views before we can reconstruct them back. This is one of those areas.

10

The End

It is time to draw this book to a close. We have discussed all that can be discussed in a manner that hopefully has not bored you, the reader, too much. As I stated in the introduction, it was my hope to bring forth my arguments for Christianity, specifically against the modern threat called progressive Christianity (or Neo-Gnosticism, as we have been calling it). I hope I have written correctly, honestly, and quickly enough that nothing felt too long. But there is one last thing I want to discuss before this book concludes.

There is one thing that I have not mentioned in all the pages that I have written, and that is the reason why, truly why, Neo-Gnostics do and believe what they do. Some can argue that they are doing this because they want to get away with sin, and that is a solid reason. Others can argue that they are naive and just do not know what the topics discussed above say—again, that is a good reason. Still others can claim that they are young and immature and that age will mature them to the ways of the world and to God. This, too, may be true. All these reasons may be good explanations of their actions and beliefs, but I think that there is one explanation that explains it better. This is that their hearts want to rebel against God. This is not a new thing, nor a revolutionary concept. Scripture speaks clearly that our hearts are wicked and that we want to, and actively do, rebel against God. What I think is happening is that since Western culture has been so overwhelmingly Christian for so long,[1] we no longer know how to deal with a culture that is striving to remove God from His throne.

Neo-Gnostics are doing what people who hate God do. They claim they are deconstructing; they claim to be searching for truth, and they claim to be trying to understand Scripture. But for the majority of them, they are not. The vast majority of Neo-Gnostics are just running from God as fast as they can. This is because they, like all of us, really, love their sin. Instead of coming to terms with our sinfulness and accepting our need for a savior, they believe that what they are doing (whatever it may be) is fine and that it is actually God or Scripture that is mistaken.

Most, if not all, Neo-Gnostics grew up in the church or in some form of Christian community. Some grew up in the overly conservative cultish side,[2] while other grew up in the overly lukewarm side. There are even some who grew up in strong Christian homes who followed Christ correctly. What I am trying to say is that it does not matter[3] how we raise our children. If they are not chosen by God, they will run and do what humans do best: resist God and despise Him.

We previously talked about how God is a loving God. Well, He is so loving that He is willing to let us pursue our own desires for destruction. If we want to follow demonic beings, sleep with tons of different people, or harm ourselves, He lets us do it. If we hate Him and want nothing to do with Him, He even lets us do that in the afterlife as well.

The point I am trying to make is this: we cannot force others to think, act, or believe the way that we want them to. There

---

[1] Basically, since the fourth century

[2] Which has produced some horrible beliefs and practices

[3] I am not saying that it does not matter how we raise our children. What I am saying is that we cannot save our children. Therefore, a child raised in the perfect home can still rebel and run from God.

are some Neo-Gnostics that do not belong to God. They will never stop fighting or hating God, and there is nothing that we can say or do to change their mind. They are repulsed by everything we stand for. They are like Emperor Julian complaining that Christians help their own sick and other people sick. They are so angry and bitter that they rather people be left alone in their misery than for a Christian to help. They are angry at their life, at society, at history, and at God. But the worst part is that they will never change their minds. They rather bathe in the muck of sin than wash off in the cleanliness of God

But there is hope. Because while there are many Neo-Gnostics who do not belong to God, there are many who do. They are just fighting Him like a tired child fighting their parent before bedtime. The amazing thing is that they will one day come to God, and that will be a glorious day. Some come to God on the His first call while others on His hundredth call. They are more like Samuel, who answered God quickly on every call. Others are more like Paul. He has to show up and blind us while we are traveling to persecute others. Either way, He gets what He wants, and we get to have our hearts turned from stone.

This is why we cannot stop preaching the gospel. This is why I wrote this book. We are called to share the gospel and make disciples. That calling is answered in many ways. Some go door to door, others travel across the globe, and still others sit down and write a book. Each way reaches a different audience or the same audience in a different way. We must continue the good fight and show the love and grace of God to others.

We cannot reach Neo-Gnostics by forcing verses in front of them. Most of the time, they have already heard them. We have to make relationships with them. Jesus did not carry the Torah around and throw it at sinners. He ate with them, He laughed with them, and He showed love and kindness. We have to do the same, partly because they are human, and that is the decent thing to do. They are people; love and befriend them. But also, that is the only way to truly evangelize. We were never called to have them pray some redemptive prayer and then walk away from them. We are called to have them enter our lives and live with them until the end. They may or may not come to the saving relationship with Christ that we hope. But it does not matter, because that is not our job. That is God's job. Our job is to include them, show them love, and maybe—just maybe—we will one day be able to call them a brother or sister in Christ.

For those who are honestly searching, I hope that this book has not come off too strong. As I mentioned in the intro, it is my desire to speak God's truth as kindly as possible. But I am human, and if my anger or pride overshadowed the message of the book, I apologize. I truly wish to see every one of you in heaven worshiping God forever. I am not quite sure how to end this, so I shall end with this: God does love you, and He wants the best for you. If you feel the tug at your heart, do not run from it. He will get His way, and His way is better than anything we can imagine. Let Him into your heart and into your life. He is a good Father who desires to bless you.[4]

Thank you for reading my book. I hope you enjoyed it and learned something useful. God bless.

---

[4] Though His idea of a blessing and ours may not match up.